Practical
Governance

Practical Governance

J. LARRY TYLER and **ERROL BIGGS**

with **LYNN KAHN**

ACHE Management Series

Health Administration Press, Chicago, Illinois

Your board, staff, or clients may also benefit from this book's insight.
For more information on quantity discounts, contact the Health
Administration Press Marketing Manager at (312) 424-9470.

06 05 04 03 02   5 4 3 2 1

Library of Congress Cataloging-in-Publication Data

Tyler, J. Larry.
    Practical governance/J. Larry Tyler and Errol Biggs.
        p. cm. — (ACHE management series)
    ISBN 1-56793-147-2 (alk. paper)
    1. Hospital trustees. 2. Health services administration. I. Biggs, Errol.
II. Title. III. Management series (Ann Arbor, Mich.)
        RA971.T954 2000
        362. 1'068'—dc21   00-061338
                                                                        CIP

The paper used in this publication meets the minimum requirements of
American National Standards for Information Sciences—Permanence of
Paper for Printed Library Materials, ANSI Z39.48–1984. ∞ ™

Health Administration Press
A division of the Foundation of the
    American College of Healthcare Executives
One North Franklin Street, Suite 1700
Chicago, IL 60606-3491
(312) 424-2800

Contents

APPENDICES

Foreword

Leland R. Kaiser, Ph.D.
President, Kaiser Consulting

THE TREMENDOUS STRENGTH and vitality of this book is revealed in its title. The book is a practical guide to governance, written for healthcare CEOs and their board members. You don't have to wade through any trivia or academic abstractions in these pages. This is a handbook full of useful ideas that are immediately applicable to your healthcare organization.

The book is written in a casual, helpful style. You can almost imagine the authors sitting around the fireplace with you, sharing their insights and observations. In fact, it is based on the actual life experiences of CEOs, board chairs, and board members of premier healthcare organizations throughout the United States. These experiences were gleaned by the authors through extensive structured interviews. The result is a kind of collective folk wisdom that is hard to find in any existing book on healthcare governance.

This book is equally suitable as part of the orientation for new board members or as a reference manual for existing trustees. It contains many handy checklists and helpful reminders. The material in the appendices is particularly valuable. You can clip it and use it with little or no modification.

Most of the governance problems I have encountered in my 30 years as a hospital consultant would never have occurred if the CEOs and board members heeded the simple guidelines and admonitions outlined in this book. What J. Larry Tyler and Errol Biggs offer us is preventive medicine for our governing bodies. In governance, as in medical care, an ounce of prevention is worth a pound of cure.

You can also use the book as a diagnostic manual for your organization. Compare your governance structure and procedures with the authors' recommendations. Is your board sick or well? How healthy is the relationship between the board and your CEO? How well does your board represent the interests and needs of the community?

Effective governance has never been so crucial as it is today. The number of people lacking adequate healthcare is growing, while the public grows increasingly skeptical about its vulnerability to managed care. Board members face intense pressure from all sides—reduced reimbursement, increased regulation, and heightened competition. The board must protect the survival of its organization and at the same time meet soaring community needs. This is no small task and it increases the stress levels experienced by board members, physicians, and CEOs.

Being a good trustee is more demanding than in previous years. The contemporary board must fulfill its mission by creating a powerful vision for the future, by involving the community in its deliberations, by encouraging collaboration among competing providers, by ensuring access to necessary capital, and by maintaining high ethical standards in all of its business practices. All of this must occur in a rapidly changing environment, where rules change frequently and instant obsolescence accompanies high innovation. This is enough to try the patience of a saint, and not all of us are saints!

Board vision, composition, education, organization, purview, and decision making are perennial challenges facing any governing body. What creates a special crisis for healthcare boards is trying to accomplish all of these traditional functions in a time of unprecedented change in delivery systems, financing, information management, and regulation. It's like jumping off a cliff in foggy conditions, with no safety net below.

What to do next? The pressures confronting management and governance require an acute sense of priorities. I believe your highest priority must be the fundamental decision you make about your organization's mission and direction. After all, your greatest challenge is to invent your preferred future in an increasingly hostile environment. This is clearly a partnership effort involving the board, management, medical staff, community, and an array of interested third-party agencies. This requires high connectivity and a sense of destiny. Creating and maintaining a sense of destiny will be made immeasurably more achievable through the wisdom assembled by Tyler and Biggs in the pages that follow. It is worth all of your hard work to achieve your vision. That is what governance is about.

Introduction

HEALTHCARE GOVERNANCE IS a profoundly different undertaking than it was even a decade ago. In the 1980s, hospital boards were charged with ensuring the continued viability of a hospital that existed ostensibly for inpatients. Today, boards that are singularly focused on such a hospital are either an anachronism or a subsidiary of a parent board whose span of control and responsibility is extensive, including managing multiple entities and a continuum of care.

Even in the face of change and regardless of the differences between organizations, some universal principles of practical governance still exist. At the same time, however, because of the dynamic nature of the healthcare marketplace, we realize that in many cases no one *right* way of governing can be followed. Therefore, CEOs and boards must make their own decisions about what does and does not work for them. Perhaps the best way to help CEOs and boards make these decisions is to present the guiding principles of practical governance, based on the experiences of CEOs and their board chairs. To this end, we interviewed a number of CEOs and many of their board chairs about their experiences in the boardroom and asked them for their counsel in light of their experiences.

This book has three major components. First, we present principles of practical governance that have withstood the test of time and that appear to be practiced by boards of leading hospitals and health systems. Second, we suggest options that can be considered as leaders grapple with such issues as board structure, board member selection and development, and the CEO's role in governance. Third, we share real-life experiences of CEOs and board chairs from all types of healthcare organizations—from expansive integrated delivery systems to rural hospitals.

As we did the research for this book, we came across a host of other excellent books that detail the nuts and bolts of effective healthcare leadership (see Appendix A). Rather than duplicate these books, we wanted to provide an "easy read" that is thought provoking and that offers practical insights to you—the reader—whether you are a CEO, a board member, or expect to hold these positions in the near future.

J. Larry Tyler, FACHE   Errol L. Biggs, PH.D., FACHE

"Universal Truths"

REGARDLESS OF THE size, location, or ownership of your organization or the structure and articulated responsibilities of your board, "universal truths" of practical governance exist. These universal truths were borne out both in our research and in our conversations with CEOs and board chairs across the country. We have categorized these truths, or tenets, as follows:

- Universal Truths for CEOs;
- Universal Truths for Board Chairs; and
- Universal Truths for Boards.

As you read further, our reasons for making these distinctions will become clear.

UNIVERSAL TRUTHS FOR CEOS

Universal Truth 1: You can never communicate too often or too much.

Any CEO who has enjoyed a positive relationship with his or her board and, more specifically, with the board chair does a substantial amount of communicating to these individuals outside of the boardroom.

We talked with one CEO who meets with his board chair and vice chair one-on-one at least every two weeks and often weekly to review the agenda for the next board meeting, to discuss any pending regulatory concerns, and so forth. He also tries to meet individually with each of the other board members at least once a month.

When CEOs communicate with their boards between board meetings they put themselves at a tremendous advantage.

We are not suggesting, however, that CEOs need to adhere to such a rigorous schedule of one-on-one meetings. In fact, unless your board is relatively small—under ten members—such frequent one-on-one meetings are probably not realistic. Rather, when CEOs communicate with their boards between board meetings they put themselves at a tremendous advantage. Informal conversations, in particular, provide CEOs an opportunity to lay out complex or controversial issues without the time constraints of a board meeting. This means that the CEOs are able to thoroughly discuss the topic at hand and to give the individual board member a chance to reflect on the conversation before the next meeting. In this way, the CEO paves the way for a more informed discussion and, more importantly, for more judicious decision making when the issue is considered by the full board.

Surprises That The Board Will Not Appreciate

- Virtually anything that has to do with unanticipated negative financial consequences
- Human resources issues that threaten to put the organization in peril—for example, allegations of sexual harassment or a looming labor dispute
- Medical staff dissatisfaction with management to the extent that they plan to act on it
- Issues that, if they hit the media, are likely to stir up negative publicity and a community backlash

Universal Truth 2: Your board does not want to be blindsided.

If you remember nothing else, remember this: Boards do not like surprises. This truth isn't rocket science, especially in the business world. Surprises breed contempt. Just think of how you have reacted when a member of your management team dropped a bomb on you. Chances are you were less than pleased.

Universal Truth 3: You serve at the pleasure of your board.

We are confident that any CEO who has lost sight of this truth one-too-many times is no longer CEO of his or her organization; as one CEO put it: "I'm the hired help." In some instances, your board chair may not be at the top of his or her game or your entire board may not see the big picture. Well, then, your job is to help them, not to step in to "save the day." In the vast majority of cases, these individuals are *volunteering* their time and energy to serve your organization. You, on the other hand, are being *paid* to guide the board in making informed decisions and to oversee the successful implementation of its directives. You may have a wonderful rapport with each board member, but if you forget the pecking order, your relationship can quickly sour and your days as CEO may be numbered. A related piece of advice: Pick your battles carefully. Occasions will arise when you feel compelled to speak up and take a stand. Just be sure that when you choose to go out on a limb, you do so for an issue or cause that is worth taking a stand on, regardless of the consequences of your action.

Universal Truth 4: You must foresee the future and help your board foresee it, too.

In most organizations, the vast majority of board members come from the community. Before they served on the board, their understanding of healthcare was likely limited to their everyday experiences. For example, although they and their families may have been covered by a managed care plan, their understanding of the implications of these plans for hospitals and physicians was likely minimal.

Just as CEOs in the 1980s had to anticipate the effect of managed care on their organizations and to focus their boards on taking appropriate action, so too must the CEO of today look forward—beyond the limited view of his or her board—to ensure that today's governance team prepares the organization for tomorrow's challenges. In other words, you need a vision and the ability to communicate it effectively to your board. Predicting the future of healthcare is far from an exact science, which leads us to the next universal truth.

Universal Truth 5: You are paid to take risks, albeit calculated risks.

Any board that thinks and says that your job is to tell it what it wants to hear is a board that will soon be governing a sinking ship. Now, at first blush, we may seem to be directly contradicting Universal Truth 3—serving at the pleasure of the board—but that is not the case. Although you should not grandstand or attempt to coerce your board in any way, the board expects you to speak up and suggest courses of action that may, on occasion, stir things up.

For example, like many other organizations a decade ago, you may have scrambled to participate in a large number of managed care contracts to protect your hospital's market share. Now, you realize that although managed care is likely here to stay, your organization must be much more selective about which plans it participates in, which is a strategic crap shoot (if such a thing exists). Certainly, if you were the CEO when your organization first entered into managed care contracts at a frenetic pace, you

The board expects you to speak up and suggest courses of action that may, on occasion, stir things up.

run the risk that the board will question why you changed your position. You could possibly "save face" by not bringing the issue to their attention. As CEO, though, saving face should never be on your list of options.

Whether or not you have a contract that offers you financial protection for risk taking, taking risks—personally and on behalf of your organization—is an inherent responsibility of your job. Phillip Goodwin, FACHE, president of Camcare, Inc., a five-hospital integrated delivery network in Charleston, West Virginia, brings this point home. At his urging, the board authorized the development of an HMO. Although the HMO had succeeded in terms of care management and per-patient cost reductions, it was a financial drain on the system. "The HMO had been bleeding the system dry," Goodwin explained. "I had to put the issue square on the table. I had to make it clear to the board that we were not going to be able to sustain the capital financing of this plan in our market. Even though I had initially pushed to acquire the HMO, I had a responsibility to now tell them we were going to have to seek an alternative."

Goodwin said that the board's reaction to his assessment was mixed—some board members disagreed; some agreed philosophically, but did not want to give up on the HMO; and some concurred entirely. "We never had open conflict, but there were definitely some pretty tense discussions. It had the potential for being one of those situations where the CEO comes back from vacation and finds out that the executive committee wants to meet with you—right away—and it isn't good news."

UNIVERSAL TRUTHS FOR BOARD CHAIRS

Universal Truth 1: Your CEO looks to you to lead the board.

During our interviews, we heard more good things than bad about our CEOs' board chairs. In some cases, our interviewees probably felt compelled to say the politically correct thing, but we got the impression that in most cases the high marks they gave their board chairs were sincere. That said, we also heard from those who said that their board chairs were "very nice people." We quickly figured out that "very nice" was code for "not terribly effective in their role." We also heard, "Well, he [or she] certainly has a strong personality," which we decoded to mean, "The board chair's leadership style is akin to a dictator's." One CEO even compared his former board chair's style to "Tito in Yugoslavia." Simply, if you are a board chair or about to become one, you need to know that the CEO wants you to lead, not acquiesce and not force feed. Yes, this is a delicate balance to strike, but a necessary one.

If you are a board chair or about to become one, you need to know that the CEO wants you to lead, not acquiesce and not force feed.

Universal Truth 2: You must do your part to cultivate an effective working relationship with the CEO.

The CEO technically works for you and the board as a whole. But the employment relationship does not mean that the CEO is solely responsible for making your relationship with each other a good one. Your responsibility extends beyond the boardroom. You must support the CEO in both formal and informal settings. On those occasions when you're at odds with the CEO, you should first discuss the conflict face-to-face and in private. Further, your CEO will likely turn to you for counsel or support throughout the course of your service. You need to be accessible and responsive. The bottom line is that if you don't do your part to cement the relationship, the repercussions will not simply affect the CEO but will carry over into the boardroom and affect the entire board's effectiveness.

Universal Truth 3: You must be a mentor.

Anyone who has served on a board for any length of time knows that board chairs vary greatly in style and effectiveness. In many cases, the board chair's attributes are learned attributes. In other words, the new chair was once a regular board member who likely observed the leadership style of the chairs who came before. That's right, people are watching. You are in the spotlight and you have the ability to influence the leadership style of future board chairs of your organization. If you are well prepared, others notice. If you are even-handed, others notice. If you are a visionary, others notice. Be all three, and the CEO and next board chair will thank you.

Universal Truth 4: Your legacy is as much what you don't do as what you do.

During our CEO interviews, we heard multiple references to the "last board chair." In many cases, those recollections were not overwhelmingly positive. We heard about board chairs who were "nice guys" and "very well liked"; but in the next breath, they were described as not terribly effective or, worse yet, not able to well prepare the board or the organization for the future. Our CEO interviewees made clear that if they had to choose between a board chair who was affable or one who made sure the tough questions were asked and addressed, they would all choose the latter type. In the final analysis, your legacy is what the board accomplishes during your tenure, or what it does not.

Universal Truth 5: You are the board's conscience.

Today, the board may face as many gray issues as it does black-and-white issues. As board chair, you have the responsibility to call it as you see it. If your board has entered, or is about to enter, a gray area with potential ethical or legal implications, you need to flag the issue and make sure the board remains on solid ground. Implicit in this role is the fact that your behavior must be beyond reproach—always. You must guard against self-dealing and conflict

People are watching. You are in the spotlight and you have the ability to influence the leadership style of future board chairs of your organization.

Your behavior must be beyond reproach—always.

of interest at all costs and make sure that you never put yourself in a position where your motives are questioned. Once again, you are a mentor and others will follow your lead—good or bad.

Never put yourself in a position where your motives are questioned.

UNIVERSAL TRUTHS FOR BOARDS

Universal Truth 1: You may be a volunteer, but your organization is counting on your commitment to the job.

As board members in today's complex healthcare environment, you face unprecedented demands on your time and energy.

In other words, don't sign on unless you are willing to put in the time between board meetings to do what is necessary to be an effective board member. Our CEO interviewees acknowledged that as board members in today's complex healthcare environment, you face unprecedented demands on your time and energy. Most of you meet as a board at least once every other month and serve on board committees that meet at least as often. But your CEOs told us that just showing up for these meetings is not enough. If you don't read your board packet in advance and if you don't pull your weight on committees, you are not only ineffective on the board, you may, in fact, be an impediment to the entire board's effectiveness.

Universal Truth 2: Your role is policy setting, not management of the organization.

This universal truth should not come as a surprise even to newcomers to the board. Yet, even though board members say they understand that they should not get involved in hospital operations, most board members at one time or another seem to wander in this direction. This propensity of some board members to get involved in issues out of their domain is actually easy to understand. As a board member, particularly one who comes from the community, you may be immersed in operational issues in the course of everyday life. You may even be somewhat of an expert on human resources issues, finance, or marketing. You have attained a comfort level with operations. But you are new to the world of healthcare and perhaps somewhat uneasy establishing policy in an arena that is not totally familiar to you, and that may be downright confusing.

As a result, you gravitate to topics and issues with which you are comfortable. Suddenly, you are involving yourself in hiring and firing decisions, in developing the organization's branding strategy, and in other issues where the CEO doesn't really want or need your input. As one CEO put it: "Some board members are like screwdrivers—everything they see looks like a screw."

Remember that your board, or a previous one, hired the CEO to manage hospital operations. If you don't believe he or she is up to the challenge, then the solution is to address that problem, not to take over the reins.

Universal Truth 3: Your personal agendas serve no one's interests, not even your own.

If you have served on a board for any length of time, you no doubt have witnessed the board member who has his or her own agenda. Sometimes the personal agenda is so glaringly apparent that the board chair, CEO, you, or another board member needs to intervene. In many cases, however, the board member's personal agenda is not necessarily a blatant conflict of interest but is inappropriate just the same. As a board member, you need to realize that when you present your own agenda, chances are everyone else in the room will realize that you are championing a personal cause, whether or not they call you on it. In other words, when you pursue a personal agenda, not only are you unlikely to emerge victorious but, worse yet, you are likely to lose credibility with your board colleagues.

> "Some board members are like screwdrivers—everything they see looks like a screw."

> Remember that your board, or a previous one, hired the CEO to manage hospital operations. If you don't believe he or she is up to the challenge, then the solution is to address that problem, not to take over the reins.

> When you pursue a personal agenda, not only are you unlikely to emerge victorious but, worse yet, you are likely to lose credibility with your board colleagues.

*Universal Truth 4: You owe it to your organization to admit
when you were wrong and to take corrective action.*

**Just as the
CEO must take
calculated risks,
so must the board.
And unless you
are clairvoyant,
you will make
some miscalcula-
tions along the
way.**

Any board that says it's batting 1,000 is probably not doing much
to lead its organization into the future. Just as the CEO must take
calculated risks, so must the board. And unless you are clairvoyant, you will make some miscalculations along the way. The
important thing to do is practice due diligence before you take
the risk, to monitor the effectiveness of your actions, and to pull
the plug when your best intentions are having damaging consequences. If you have any doubt that this is the right course of
action, just reflect on how you feel when government policy-
makers let "the wheels fall off the bus" before they admit they
were wrong and take corrective action. Besides creating ill will,
this approach is, at its extreme, a tremendous breach of the board's
fiduciary responsibility. It's ill advised, imprudent, and just bad
governance.

**If your organiza-
tion loses the trust
of the community,
your organization
sooner or later
will pay the price.**

*Universal Truth 5: You must not lose sight of the community;
boards that do fail their organizations.*

This universal truth does not apply only to not-for-profit healthcare organizations; it applies equally to those in the investor-
owned sector. Some boards are almost always focused on the
community. Still others become so immersed in the intricacies
of governing a complex healthcare organization that they lose
sight of the implications of their decisions on the communities
their organizations serve. The danger of such myopic vision is
obvious: If your organization loses the trust of the community,
your organization sooner or later will pay the price. Whether you
start losing patients, your stock price declines, your endowments
diminish, or your medical staff reduces its admissions to your
hospital, the consequences won't be pleasant.

These are only a handful of the universal truths of practical governance. We could have highlighted many more—perhaps even enough for an entire book. These universal truths may appear to be largely negative or accusatory in nature, and perhaps there is some truth in that. But many of these truths have come to light through our research.

The good news is that plenty of boards are models for practical governance. The CEO, board chair, and board as a whole understand their respective roles and execute them well. We share their stories in the chapters that follow.

2

The CEO's Role

In CHAPTER 1, we identified five universal truths for CEOs. In summary, the CEO must:

1. communicate effectively and frequently;
2. avoid suddenly springing information on the board;
3. recognize that he or she serves at the pleasure of the board;
4. be a visionary and inspire the board with that vision; and
5. take calculated risks.

In this chapter, we explore each truth in greater detail.

THE GREAT COMMUNICATOR

Being an effective communicator may be more art than science, but in the case of communicating formally with the board, the CEO should have some standardized mechanisms in place to ensure the timely flow of "need-to-know" information. To this end, let's focus first on arguably the most essential CEO-board tool of communication: the board meeting agenda packet.

Board Agenda Packet

If your process for developing and disseminating materials for your board meetings is not like a well-oiled machine, you're

Exhibit 2.1: Agenda Packet Checklist

- Did I discuss the agenda with my board chair before finalizing?
- Did my board receive the materials sufficiently before the meeting to allow for thorough review? (Ideally, the board should receive the packet at least a week in advance.)
- Does the agenda clearly point to the items that require board action?
- If issues that the board has not addressed are on the agenda, are materials that provide sufficient and balanced background on the issue(s) enclosed?
- Are the financials timely, accurate, and understandable?
- Does the packet contain reports started months or even years ago that are no longer relevant?
- Are all of the enclosed memos and reports clearly written and to the point? (We have known CEOs who boasted about the number of tabs and the weight of their board packets. Although the CEOs may be impressed with the magnitude of their agenda packets, chances are their boards won't be. The key is not to *underwhelm* or *overwhelm* the board with information.)

ready for a tune up. Perhaps the best way to assess the caliber of your board meeting packet is to routinely ask yourself key questions, see Exhibit 2.1, that would help you determine the appropriateness of the board's agenda packet. See Appendix B for a sample board meeting agenda from Memorial Health System.

You have a responsibility to produce board materials that, at a minimum, meet the criteria in Exhibit 2.1. To the extent that you can make other enhancements, so much the better. For example, many CEOs now include a quarterly or annual report of key financial and quality indicators of organizational performance in their board packets. (Given that the Joint Commission on Accreditation of Health Care Organizations requires that boards be involved in improving performance, we believe such quality reports should be required for inclusion in packets.)

We want to emphasize that board meetings should be held no more than six times annually. If you think that your full board needs to meet more frequently, we recommend that you revisit your process for getting board work done. Chances are that you have not effectively delegated work to committees and subcommittees or that you are asking the board to consider issues that can be appropriately handled elsewhere.

Day-to-Day Communications

As CEO, your informal communications are just as important as your formal communications. Your ability to stay "connected" to the staff, including the medical staff, is critical to your effectiveness as a conduit between the organization and the board. You want to be accessible and approachable to catch wind of issues before they become larger than life. You want to run interference so that issues that should never come to the board's attention are addressed expeditiously by you or your staff. You want to present yourself as your staff's biggest advocate—and truly be that individual—but you must do so in a way that does not diminish your responsibilities to the organization as a whole.

Most CEOs say that they understand the importance of their informal communications with staff. They perceive themselves as accessible and responsive individuals. Unfortunately, many CEOs need a reality check. The truth is that many CEOs are weighed down by a multitude of demands and pressures and tend to be accessible and responsive only when they have time. As a result, informal communication quickly moves down on their list of priorities—that is, until they are blindsided by an issue that makes its way to the board without their knowledge.

One CEO we spoke with recalled when this scenario happened to him. Suddenly, the executive committee of his board held a meeting with his medical staff leadership *without* him. The medical staff leaders called the meeting to appeal to the

Many CEOs now include a quarterly or annual report of key financial and quality indicators of organizational performance in their board packets.

Your ability to stay "connected" to the staff, including the medical staff, is critical to your effectiveness as a conduit between the organization and the board.

board to fire the CEO because they had lost faith in him. The board in this case probably should not have agreed to the meeting, particularly without inviting the CEO to attend. Luckily for the CEO, despite the apparent breach of protocol, the executive committee stood behind him. After this harrowing experience, you can bet that the CEO moved informal communication up on his list of priorities.

So how do you know whether your informal communications are effective or somehow lacking? Typically, your management team knows, although it isn't necessarily comfortable with sharing its observations with you, particularly when it thinks you could be doing better. If you truly want to know how you are doing and are prepared to make improvements as indicated, you may want to consider using an assessment tool or a multirater instrument for 360-degree feedback. This is a process whereby you, your board, and your management team all assess your leadership effectiveness and communication style. You may find that your perceptions are not shared. (See Chapter 10 for more on CEO performance appraisal.)

Informal Communications with Board Members

As noted in Chapter 1, CEOs who enjoy positive relationships with their boards are CEOs who take the time to talk with their board members outside of meetings. Certainly, having weekly or perhaps even monthly one-on-one meetings with your board is unrealistic, unless the board is relatively small. But even one-on-one meetings once a year with each board member can be extremely beneficial. Conversely, if the only time board members get a chance to talk with you is in the boardroom, you are making a mistake.

The vast majority of your board members give their time and energy to your organization because they believe in it and want to make a positive difference on behalf of the community they serve. Similarly, they need to know that you care as much as they do. If they see you only in the boardroom, your commitment will be much tougher to sell.

If you are a new CEO, sit down with as many board members as possible before your first board meeting. Sure this meeting will eat up a lot of time—time you would rather devote to getting up to speed on a multitude of things. It will be time well spent, however, because you get a firsthand understanding of the personalities and priorities of individual board members. You also want to begin to get a sense of which board members are leaders and which are followers.

Veteran CEOs will advise you to make time—not just initially, but routinely—for your board chairs. In other words, carve out time to review the upcoming board agenda with your chairs before each meeting; schedule a standing lunch or at least a standing phone call at least once a month, or more frequently if your board meets more often than every other month; and be accessible every minute, day and night. Although, as we mentioned earlier, you serve at the pleasure of your board, the board chairs we interviewed all said that they consider support for the CEO a big part of their job. The only way they can do that effectively is by talking with you, learning from you about operational implications of past or potential policy decisions, and believing that you truly value their counsel.

THE NO-SURPRISE SCHOOL OF LEADERSHIP

In today's healthcare organizations, deciding on which issues to bring to the board's attention and when the appropriate time to do so is not always easy. First-time CEOs find this determination to be particularly challenging and often err on the side of asking for board involvement in decisions that are much too operational

> The vast majority of your board members give their time and energy to your organization because they believe in it and want to make a positive difference on behalf of the community they serve.

in nature. (A few decision-making meetings with the board about paint colors for the nursery or menu planning for a hospital fundraiser quickly cure this tendency.)

The other extreme case is when the CEO operates under the dangerous misconception that he or she knows best in virtually all situations and involves the board only in the purest policy issues. Certainly, the board's job is to set policy, not to become involved in operations. But some issues are in that gray zone—they may first appear as operational issues but, upon closer inspection, do in fact have policy implications. Take, for example, a labor dispute. Labor disputes typically begin because some employees are unhappy with compensation, benefits, or other aspects of their job. At first, dissatisfaction may be voiced informally and make its way to the CEO anecdotally. In some of these cases, concerns can be addressed by management without the board's knowledge or input. But if the grievances are numerous and the dissatisfaction is widespread, chances are that a quick fix won't work. As CEO, you can bide your time and see if things quiet down; after all, if all is well, you "saved" the board from having to spend time on this troublesome issue. But while you are biding your time, your disgruntled workers may be hard at work—not necessarily at their jobs but at making their concerns heard, and not just in the boardroom, but out there in the community. It would be a shame—perhaps even a career-limiting move for you—if your board learned about the employee unrest at a dinner party or in the local newspaper.

A labor dispute is just one example of the type of in-house information you want to think long and hard about *not* sharing with your board. As a rule, we recommend that you ask yourself the questions in Exhibit 2.2 when deciding if an issue you're dealing with is one that the board should hear about. If you answer "yes" to all or most of the questions, think before excluding the issue from the board agenda.

> **Exhibit 2.2: Questions To Help You Determine If An Issue Needs To Be Shared With The Board**
>
> - Does the issue have the potential to become explosive?
> - Is the board likely to learn about the issue from others—either from others on my staff or others in the community?
> - Will the effective resolution of the issue possibly require policy changes?
> - Has the issue surfaced before and has it benefited from board attention in the past?
> - Am I reluctant to bring the issue to the board's attention because the fact that it is an issue may reflect badly on me?

Don't ever lose sight of your place in the pecking order .... Yes, you are paid to lead; but you are also paid to follow the board's lead.

Obviously, we are strong proponents of the "no-surprise school of leadership." No CEO ever lost his or her job, at least not that we are aware of, for sharing too much with his or her board. In contrast, plenty of former CEOs had to move on because their boards were surprised one-too-many times.

WHO'S THE BOSS?

Don't ever lose sight of your place in the pecking order. Although the vast majority of board members wholeheartedly want to support you, you don't have carte blanche. Yes, you are paid to lead; but you are also paid to follow the board's lead. You may not always agree with the direction in which the board has you headed, and, clearly, you have a right, albeit a responsibility, to speak up in such cases. But, ultimately, if the board charts a course and you choose not to follow, you have only yourself to blame for the potential consequences.

Without exception, all of the CEOs we interviewed seemed to clearly understand the concept of serving at the board's pleasure. And, interestingly, all of the board chairs we interviewed really downplayed their "implicit power" over their CEOs. We suggest that in the vast majority of cases, you can depend on your board's support because your board members trust you and believe that you want to do the right thing. But cross the line and lose sight of your role, and the dynamics are likely to change quite quickly. Only the lucky few learn from their boards that they have overstepped their bounds before it is too late.

THE VISIONARY CEO

Are you a visionary? As CEO, you had better be. Your board does not expect you to be clairvoyant, but it does expect you to lead it into the future because of your firsthand understanding of the healthcare marketplace. Remember, most of your board members are not intimately familiar with the issues of the day. Even your more senior board members probably have considerably less insight into the complexities of the issues they must address.

Given that you are the resident expert, your responsibility is to try to anticipate the future. In fact, your board is counting on it. Fred Wolf, immediate past chair at Steamboat Springs Health Care Association, which owns Yampa Valley Medical Center, in Steamboat Springs, Colorado, put it this way: "You can have the best board in the world, but if they don't have someone in there as CEO that can run the place with an eye on the future, the organization is going to suffer."

YOU CAN'T ALWAYS PLAY IT SAFE

Certainly, as CEO you have a responsibility to keep your organization on a steady course. You want to articulate a vision that your board can embrace and your staff can work toward. Schizophrenic leadership—that is, a vision that constantly fluctuates—breeds confusion and undermines others' confidence in you.

"You can have the best board in the world, but if they don't have someone in there as CEO that can run the place with an eye on the future, the organization is going to suffer."

—Fred Wolf

That said, you are also the individual who is best positioned to propose bold new directions for your organization. You are in this unique position for simple reasons. First, as CEO you obviously understand healthcare and its intricacies. Second, you have a firsthand understanding of the strengths and weaknesses of your organization.

More than anyone else on your board or on your staff, you have, or should have, a "big-picture" understanding of your organization and its need to flourish in the future. With this knowledge comes responsibility—a responsibility to identify new initiatives that will help fortify your organization for the future.

The vast majority of healthcare CEOs in the United States have an employment contract (see Appendix J). This contract is your insurance policy for risk taking. The good news is that in most cases if you have taken your board and your organization down the wrong path, but not because of negligence on your part, no retribution for your miscalculation will follow you. Your job may not be on the line or, if it is, you have a severance package in place that offers a measure of security.

The flip side is that you can play it safe. Ironically, playing it safe by not taking risks probably puts you in even greater peril. If you perpetuate the status quo, you may be fine for the present; but chances are your organization is not going to be positioned well for the future. So even if your current board is satisfied with your leadership, you run the risk that a future board will question why you didn't do more to keep the organization on a forward course.

Taking risks is risky. But we believe that not taking risks is even riskier. Given our view, we recommend that you routinely ask yourself the questions in Exhibit 2.3.

If you have trouble answering the last question, you must do some soul searching. You need to explore why you might not want to discuss these issues with the board. If your reluctance comes primarily from the unpleasantness of the topic or if you

Exhibit 2.3: Questions To Help You Determine Your Organization's Readiness for Risk Taking

1. Am I aware of national, regional, or local trends that have the potential to affect my organization?
2. How entrenched is my organization in its current way of doing things? Are we flexible enough to respond quickly to changing market forces?
3. In what ways is my organization vulnerable or potentially vulnerable, and what actions could we take to fortify our position?
4. Should I present these issues and potential solutions to the board for consideration?

are concerned that the board won't buy into your proposed solutions, then you probably need to force yourself out of your comfort zone. Do your homework, look at the issue from all sides, and then broach the issue with your board chair. Your reluctance may turn out to be a Pandora's Box, but it may be one that had to be opened.

A final word of advice to CEOs: Although your job shouldn't be your life, the city or town in which your hospital is located should be your *home.* In other words, if you take a CEO job with the attitude that you are just "passing through" on the way to bigger and better things, it will be noticed. This word of advice comes from Terry Gerber, chair of the board at Memorial Health System in South Bend, Indiana, as he reflected on Memorial's CEO, Philip Newbold, FACHE: "When you have a CEO coming and going from different systems—meaning they already think they are going somewhere else—the result will not be nearly as good as if the CEO adopts the community. Maybe they didn't feel this way initially, but I can tell you today that Phil and his wife consider South Bend their home. Because a CEO who sees the community as his or her home wants the organization to reflect the values of the community, and it shows."

You may be wondering how boards feel about their CEOs. That is hard to say. We do know, however, that most healthcare system and hospital CEOs *believe* that their governing boards support their work. That's according to a recent survey of 214 CEOs whose hospitals participate in a San Diego-based purchasing alliance. Ninety-five percent of the CEOs *believe* that their boards support them. We hope they are right.

3
The Board Chair's Role

IN CHAPTER 1, we identified five universal truths for board chairs. In summary, the board chair must:

1. lead the board;
2. cultivate an effective working relationship with the CEO;
3. mentor others on the board;
4. be decisive and move the board to action; and
5. walk the straight and narrow.

In this chapter, we explore each truth in greater detail.

LEADING NOT COMMANDEERING

Your leadership style as board chair is greatly influenced by your leadership style outside of the boardroom. If you tend to command and control, chances are that is how you run board meetings. Realistically, nothing we say in this book will influence you to make a profound difference in your style. But at the risk of preaching, we think you should know that if you lead by "command and control," you probably are significantly detracting from the quality of your board meetings and hindering effective decision making.

Harry Duncanson, chair of the board of commissioners at Memorial Healthcare System in Hollywood, Florida, recalled a previous board chair whose ego got the best of him and the board: "This board chair was more impressed with himself than he was mindful of the job he was supposed to be doing. If you treat people in an authoritative manner, like he did, I don't think you get the same kind of communication that you do when you treat people with respect. You have to consider that people look up to you not because of your title, but because of the role you have in serving the community."

Some CEOs believe that their board chairs—either past or present—know only how to lead by force and in most cases aren't even aware that they are doing so. If you are curious about the impression your "style" makes on your CEO and board, ask yourself the questions in Exhibit 3.1.

> **Exhibit 3.1: Questions To Help You Become Aware of Your Leadership Style**
>
> - Do I come into board meetings knowing what decisions the board should reach on a particular issue(s)?
> - Do I typically tell my CEO what needs to be done before the board meeting at which the issue is scheduled to be discussed?
> - Is my board generally conciliatory and willing to follow my lead with few questions?
> - Do I often discourage questions so that we don't fall behind on the agenda?

If you answer "yes" to even one of the questions, you must do some serious introspection. You certainly can't be accused of not making things happen at board meetings, but chances are your colleagues and CEO find you heavy handed at best and perhaps even autocratic.

Based on their years of experience with a wide variety of board chairs, our CEO interviewees told us that the truly effective board chair has leadership ability that is built on a solid foundation of knowledge of the organization and its issues, has a genuine respect for the CEO and board, and recognizes that he or she alone does not have all the answers. Equally important, if not more so, is the vision the board chair brings to the board and the adeptness with which he or she helps the board translate that vision into a reality.

John McNeil, CEO of North Hawaii Community Hospital in Kamuela, Hawaii, said this about his board chair: "When we first asked him to join the board he said, 'If you want me for my money, I have all the charities I need already. But if you want me for my vision and if you think I can help you, I will join.' Without question, it is his vision that has been the greatest value."

McNeil was referring to the vision of Earl Bakken, president emeritus, board of directors at North Hawaii Community Hospital. It was a vision that Bakken said he kept very much alive during his term as board chair, and one that the current chair continues to champion today. We believe Bakken's vision is noteworthy because of its breadth, whether or not you buy into it. It is a vision for the organization, but it is much more—it is a vision for improving community health. Bakken's vision is built on the premise that our healthcare system should concentrate on controlling the demand for healthcare rather than controlling the supply of healthcare. It is a vision for building healthy communities and is predicated on six tenets:

1. Communities need resource centers that help people become involved in their own healthcare and achieve healthy lifestyles.
2. Hospitals need to integrate, not simply offer, high-tech and high-touch services that address the body, mind, and spirit.
3. Communities must mentor the young and teach them about the dangers of drugs and violence and inspire them to live healthy lives.

4. Communities must provide jobs for everyone because poverty leads to many of our healthcare problems.
5. Healthcare organizations must work toward more equitable reimbursement for services (Bakken championed medical savings accounts in particular).
6. Healthcare organizations must measure their effectiveness as it relates to building healthy communities.

Bakken said his board embraced this vision, and it provided a context for virtually all that the board did. But did the vision translate into reality? "Is the hospital and the community there yet? No, of course not. But they are getting there slowly and have made and continue to make some real progress," Bakken explained.

Whether or not your vision is as comprehensive as Bakken's, you must demonstrate to your board that you will lead the way as it navigates the murky waters ahead. How does this vision play out in the boardroom? Here are a few noticeable indications that the board chair is leading effectively in the boardroom:

- A high level of participation by most or all of the board members;
- An involved CEO who interjects comments and information that will assist the board in its deliberations;
- An all-around comfort level among board members with voicing unpopular decisions;
- Sufficient time for meaningful discussion;
- Limited tolerance for tangential discussions or personal agendas; and
- Thoughtful decision making.

If your board meetings reflect these attributes, chances are that you are leading effectively. You have mastered a critical part of your job. Another critical responsibility is to build a strong working relationship with your CEO. As board chair, the quality of your relationship is as much your responsibility as it is the CEO's.

ARE YOU ON THE SAME PAGE?

Not surprisingly, all of the CEOs we interviewed described their relationship with their board chairs as "very good" or something close to that description. That's not surprising; after all, to say otherwise could be a career-limiting move for the speaker. We did our best to read "between the lines" so that we could provide insight into what you bring, or should bring, to your relationship with your CEO. Your responsibilities, at least as CEOs see it, include the following.

Accessibility

Your CEO is well aware that your day-to-day responsibilities compete for your time. That said, the CEO believes that if you agree to serve as board chair, you must make time to talk with him or her as needed between board meetings so that the CEO can update you on issues that have emerged since the last board meeting. At the same time, your CEO recognizes that your time should be used judiciously, not on issues that you are paying the CEO to address as CEO.

Jim Marley, board chair of PinnacleHealth System, where John Cramer, FACHE, is president and CEO, in Harrisburg, Pennsylvania, told us he takes this responsibility to his CEO seriously. "I feel a high level of responsibility when it comes to ensuring that John and I are working closely together. I understand the problems he faces and do what I can to provide experience, insight, and guidance that can help him. I try to get together with John about every two weeks for a 'catch-up discussion' about what's happening, where we stand on various issues, and

> **The CEO believes that if you agree to serve as board chair, you must make time to talk with him or her as needed between board meetings.**

so forth. The bottom line is that I feel I have to be available if he needs to talk with me or needs my help."

Input

Most CEOs we interviewed said that they typically take board agendas to their board chair for comment before dissemination to the full board. CEOs aren't looking for a rubber stamp. They want you to speak up when the board agenda does not include everything you think it should. CEOs hate when you notice holes in the agenda once you are already in the boardroom because that's too little, too late.

Candor

CEOs wouldn't be CEOs if they didn't have battle scars. They have almost certainly been roughed up during the course of their careers. You don't need to sugar coat anything on their account. They want you to play it straight. If you think they are veering off course, tell them. If you think they are overlooking an issue that needs to be addressed, tell them. If you think they are not meeting board expectations, tell them. Tell them before they undergo their annual performance evaluation. You are not doing the organization or the CEO a favor by keeping quiet.

Respect

Either the current board or a previous board hired the CEO; therefore, that hiring decision was most likely made carefully, very carefully. Assuming that was the case, then the CEO is some-one who was considered competent to do the job. Although you may not personally like the CEO or perhaps do not agree with all

---

Margin notes:

CEOs aren't looking for a rubber stamp. They want you to speak up when the board agenda does not include everything you think it should.

CEOs wouldn't be CEOs if they didn't have battle scars. You don't need to sugar coat anything on their account. They want you to play it straight.

Although you may not personally like the CEO or perhaps do not agree with all of the decisions he or she makes, you owe it to the organization and the individual to show respect for the CEO.

of the decisions he or she makes, you owe it to the organization and the individual to show respect for the CEO. Failure to do so will reflect badly on you and the organization. The CEO will pick up on your lack of respect and so will the board. Where does that leave you? Quite simply, you will be left with a CEO who feels second-guessed and a board that, for all intents and purposes, is dysfunctional or on the road to being so. Certainly, if the CEO is truly not up to the task, and that is the view of the board, you need to make a change. Short of that, though, you have a responsibility to demonstrate your respect.

If you move the board and the organization forward during your term, your successors will recognize that they need to do the same.

OTHERS ARE WATCHING

Before you became a board chair, you were probably a regular member of the board with a front-row seat to view the board chair in action. You saw the board chair at his or her best—and worst. Now, you are in the spotlight and others are watching you. Your board's next chair, in particular, is probably watching you quite intently.

Because you are teaching others by example, you can pave the way for years of practical governance or, of course, just the opposite. If you come to board meetings prepared and familiar with the agenda, you are sending a message: This is what board chairs do. If you advocate full board participation in discussion, this message will be communicated, too. If you move the board and the organization forward during your term, your successors will recognize that they need to do the same.

You have a wonderful opportunity to set an example. If you embrace that opportunity, the next board chair will thank you, the board will thank you, and the CEO will thank you. If you don't, you may not personally suffer the consequences because your board service is over, but the board and the organization may suffer the consequences for years to come.

STILL WATERS CAN SINK YOU

The last chapter talked about the CEO's role as a risk taker. Similarly, as board chair you must guard against being risk averse. Further, you may never be immortalized in your role by the organization, but you certainly want to be remembered as someone who made a positive difference.

One way to accomplish this is to establish your priorities as chair before you assume office and to announce them to the board once you begin your term. Ideally, you will want to establish those priorities in conjunction with the CEO. The CEO can help crystallize the pressing issues and provide suggestions for your selection. For example, one board chair we know decided that one of his priorities would be to revitalize the organization's strategic planning process so that it was more meaningful to those involved and more useful to the organization than past plans had been.

If your style or your desire is not to formally establish priorities, make sure nevertheless that you convey early in your term of service that you are not there to perpetuate the status quo. You can make this point effectively in a number of ways by:

- encouraging the board to consider all sides of the issues;
- moving the board along the continuum to action; and
- taking the initiative in presenting the tough issues.

These last two items need further comment. Many of our CEO interviewees said that one of the most frustrating problems for them is when they leave board meetings without reaching decisions on crucial issues. One of the reasons you are there as board chair is to make sure this doesn't occur. If you let the board meander from issue to issue, never reaching closure on them, then what real contribution have you made? Your legacy should

Your legacy should not be that you were a swell person, but that you were masterful at getting the board to work together to reach informed decisions.

not be that you were a swell person, but that you were masterful at getting the board to work together to reach informed decisions.

Again, at the risk of preaching, we want to underscore the importance of being a board chair who does indeed make sure that tough issues are discussed and resolved, even if the issues revolve around a difference of opinion between the board and the CEO. Margaret Sabin, whom we interviewed when she was CEO of Yampa Valley Medical Center, which is owned by the not-for-profit corporation Steamboat Springs Health Care Association, in Steamboat Springs, Colorado but is now CEO of Marin Health Center in San Rafael, California, recalled that the CEO who preceded her told of a board chair who fell short in this regard. "He said the board felt like they were on quicksand—not sure where they stood much of the time," Sabin said. "I know from experience that CEOs and boards are both a lot more comfortable with a board chair who just puts the issue out there."

ARE YOU BEYOND REPROACH?

Most boards have systems in place, such as conflict-of-interest policies, to guard against self-dealing on the part of their board members. (See Appendix C for a sample conflict-of-interest policy.) These systems tend to work well when the potential conflict of interest is black and white. For example, at Yampa Valley Medical Center, the conflict-of-interest policy alleviates the vast majority of potential missteps by board members. Yampa Valley's former CEO Sabin said: "It is important to have a clear policy that says that if a board member enters into a role where he or she is compensated by any relationship that might affect his or her objectivity on a particular matter, the [member] is required to disclose the potential conflict to the board. For example, if a board member owns a construction company and your hospital is soliciting bids to build a new wing, the policy must be followed.

If the board decides a board member's business interest is not a conflict of interest, then the board member is clear to participate in the decision-making process. Board members generally respect the policy, and the process works."

It is not okay on any occasion to champion a personal cause.

If you have served on a board in any industry for any length of time, however, you know that many issues are not that clear cut and that self-interest is unfortunately alive and well in the world of governance. As the board chair, you must assiduously avoid these gray zones. Even the slightest hint that you are crossing the line could be disastrous.

Any appearance of an ethical breach on your part can have a serious negative impact on others' perceptions of you. Worse yet, it can, by implication, signify that although out-and-out ethical breaches are not tolerated, championing a personal cause occasionally is "okay" with you.

Clearly, it is not okay on any occasion to champion a personal cause. Instead, as board chair the message you must consistently send and hold as sacrosanct is that the board is there to serve the organization and the community the organization serves. Self-service, no matter how incidental, is in reality a disservice.

4

The Board's Role

IN CHAPTER 1, we identified five universal truths for boards. In summary, the boards must:

1. demonstrate commitment to the job;
2. set policy, not oversee day-to-day operations;
3. guard against self-dealing;
4. take corrective action when necessary; and
5. stay focused on community needs.

In this chapter, we explore each truth in greater detail.

THIS IS VOLUNTEERING?

Perhaps the most unexpected aspect of serving on a healthcare board is that the prestige of the position is more often than not overshadowed by the position's demands. In other words, if you are looking to serve on a board to receive affirmation that you have "arrived," we recommend that you steer clear of a hospital or system board. Camcare's Phillip Goodwin agreed: "You have to understand that this is a real job. You're not here to have fun. You have a major contribution to make, and it may be really tough."

John Jeter, M.D., president and CEO of Hays Medical Center in Hays, Kansas, went even further: "Board members really have to dedicate themselves to learning our business. That is the only way they are going to be effective. If they can't make that commitment, we don't want them. This is going to be the most demanding board position they've ever held, but it is also going to be the most rewarding."

CEOs noted that their interest was more in the board members' commitment to their work than in the number of hours they logged.

Virtually all of the CEOs we interviewed emphasized that they have worked with a number of board members who received a rude awakening upon realizing that their service on the board would require them to attend up to a dozen committee meetings a year in addition to six or so board meetings. They were even more surprised to learn that the committees were actually expected to do "real" work, like exploring and discussing issues before a full board meeting so that the issues could be presented to the board with recommendations and could be handled expeditiously. (See Appendix D for a sample list of board member responsibilities.)

We asked CEOs and board chairs to estimate the number of hours per month, on average, that their board members should be spending on board-related business. Their answers ranged from 5 to 15 hours, excluding attendance at committee meetings, board meetings, and other hospital-sponsored events in the community. Our interviewees said that the number of hours can increase significantly when the board is faced with a "crisis"—for example, a financial downturn.

But our CEOs, in particular, noted that their interest was more in the board members' commitment to their work than in the number of hours they logged. One system CEO, who has worked with scores of board members over the years, put it this way: "Board members rip open the agenda packet as they walk into the board meeting and basically bail at the first unhappy words that come from a doc. Those are the good ones. The bad ones are trying to rip you off and get, let's say, all the insurance business or

[the] financial advisor role. I think most CEOs feel that it is a bit like democracy — they don't have a better alternative, but the current system isn't very good. I would say I have an above-average board, and it's still pretty bad."

What's the bottom line? Quite simply, if you aren't serious about serving the organization and demonstrating your commitment through hard, selfless work, this isn't the volunteer role for you. Instead, you may want to consider taking on a less-demanding role on the board.

LET SOMEONE ELSE PICK THE PAINT COLOR

Policy setting can be more amorphous and considerably less enjoyable than choosing paint colors for the new pediatric wing. Unfortunately, your board role is the former. The CEO knows that and most board chairs know that. If you are a board member, you probably also know that. But some CEOs contend that a disconnect often exists between what you know and what you do.

Richard Knapp, PH.D., board chair of INOVA Health System in Fairfax, Virginia, attested to this phenomenon: "It is much easier to discuss what kind of asphalt we're going to use on the driveway or who is going to be hired to run a particular department than it is to think about where we want the organization to be in ten years. But that's a hard job, and people frequently retreat to talking about the concrete. I try to keep them focused on questions like 'Where are we going?', 'What's going on next year?', 'What do we want to be?' These are all answerable questions, but you have to recognize two things. First, some problems never go away, and you need to keep working on them. The other thing is that there is no such thing as 'getting there.' The current environment requires that we understand the organization is in a constant state of *becoming.*"

We found two primary reasons why boards stray into operations and away from policy. First, as we noted above, addressing operational matters is considerably easier than addressing policy issues. Many board members spend their professional lives in operations-related roles. They've been there, they've done that. For example, board members who are CPAs may want to get immersed in the minutia of the hospital's financial statements, construction company owners may want hands-on involvement in building projects, and so on.

How prevalent is this problem? Well, apparently quite prevalent—enough that it was the subject of a 1999 article in *Harvard Business Review*. In the article "Working on Nonprofit Boards: Don't Assume the Shoe Fits," author F. Warren McFarlan wrote: "Most businesspeople will serve on the board of a nonprofit organization at some point. But the governance of nonprofits can differ dramatically from the governance of businesses. Even the best intentions can prove disastrous when new board members fail to understand that their traditional business experience can carry them only so far." The same rationale is true for healthcare boards.

What is the potential negative impact when a board becomes immersed in operations? North Hawaii Community Hospital's John McNeil said: "The moment the board tells the CEO what to do, the board loses power because no one can hold the CEO accountable for the outcome. And even worse, if the board tells a staff member what to do, the board has really cut off its power. It is a bad situation all around."

Certainly, it is understandable that board members would want action and want it quickly when they determine, for example, that a hospital executive is not making the grade. That is not an unreasonable expectation. The problem is that board members often cross the line between expecting the CEO to act and taking action themselves. In some cases, CEOs or board chairs are successful in redirecting the board before they go down this road. But our CEO interviewees admitted that when board members have so much momentum, getting them back on track becomes virtually impossible.

> "The governance of nonprofits can differ dramatically from the governance of businesses."
>
> —F. Warren McFarlan

Beside the boards' admitted comfort level with operations, sometimes they become immersed in operations for another reason: They have lost faith in the CEO.

We would argue, though, that in the vast majority of cases, the board's involvement in picking paint colors or conducting executive performance appraisals has little to do with its lack of faith in the CEO's ability to manage the organization. Frankly, even if the board's operations bent is a reflection of its dissatisfaction with the CEO, it should still not be focused on operations; it should be focused on finding a new CEO. As one board member put it: "A board member should remember NIFO—nose in, fingers out!"

Before you reach the conclusion that your CEO isn't "the right fit," as a board member you must make sure to understand the CEO's role, not just the day-to-day responsibilities but in the boardroom. One of our CEO interviewees put it this way: "I think boards really need to understand that the old three-legged stool concept—CEO, board chair, medical staff leader—is a pernicious one. The reality today is that the stool has only two legs. One leg represents the board and management, who support the organization's principle and are its agents. The other leg represents the physicians, who have their own economic interests. It is a very direct, albeit arms-length, relationship. In other words, management is not some third party, it is the board's agent."

Unfortunately, too many boards fail to understand the CEO's role as a negotiator. They either fault the CEO for "selling out" or "they applaud" the CEO's hard line while the medical staff seethes. Knox Singleton, CEO of INOVA Health System, put it this way: "I think boards can sometimes be a little unrealistic about the conflict inherent in economic relationships between the hospital and the medical staff. Because boards do not have a significant personal stake in the game the way management and the medical staff do, they tend to want everyone to be 'happy,' when that's not realistic—at least not in the short term. The more that board members look at the hospital's resources as if it were their own money, the more realistic they will be about the nature of essential working relationships within the organization they govern."

Secure and effective CEOs are not looking for boards who are cheerleaders. You are on the board as a steward of the organization, and in that capacity your duty is to ask the tough questions. Dan Coleman, president and CEO of John C. Lincoln Health Network in Phoenix, Arizona, put it this way: "I believe that one of the worst enemies of governance is when the board doesn't ask questions and doesn't express concerns. I have a problem when board members don't ask the tough questions. Some of the best things my organization has done have been prompted by one board member who dared to speak up and ask a question while the rest of the group was going in a different direction."

THIS ISN'T ABOUT YOU

During the course of our interviews, we heard a few horror stories about board members who engaged in self-dealing. All of our interviewees said that their organizations have conflict-of-interest policies, and most said that at the start of each board meeting board members are asked to disclose any potential conflict of interest with the agenda items to be discussed.

Further, a number of CEOs said that they are thankful that they rarely have to serve as the board's conscience. In addition, they said their boards do an excellent job of self-policing—that is, speaking up when another board member appears to have a vested interest in the issue at hand.

But on occasion, conflict-of-interest matters do get dicey; as one CEO interviewee recalled: "[One of my] past board members is an attorney. His firm was actually retained by a couple of our physicians to work on a dispute we had on a general partnership back in the 1980s. An attorney from the board member's firm came to meet with me and the physician. He said, 'I'm not here as an attorney—I'm here as a friend to both of you.' It was pretty evident

> Secure and effective CEOs are not looking for boards who are cheerleaders. You are on the board as a steward of the organization, and in that capacity your duty is to ask the tough questions.

that he wanted to steer the situation. It got contentious and we started entering into correspondence. When I brought the issue to the board, I included copies of his correspondence. The board member claimed that he didn't know that somebody else in his firm had taken on this matter. It was a blatant lie, and ultimately he had to declare a conflict of interest at the board meeting."

In this case, because the board member was politically appointed, forcing his hand to get him to resign from the board was not possible. But the CEO told us that despite the member's political backing, the organization had enough support to keep him from serving another term.

Certainly, situations like this are the exception to the rule. Nevertheless, keep in mind that as a board member, you represent the organization and the community, not yourself. Further, you are surrounded by individuals who have a common goal—to represent the best interests of the organization and the community. This goal is the core of practical governance. If they see that you have a personal agenda, you will, at the least, become *persona non grata* and, worse, perhaps even be forced to retire from board service.

> As a board member, you represent the organization and the community, not yourself.

GET OVER IT

Just because you serve on a board doesn't mean you have all the answers. What your organization expects of you is judicious decision making—making the best decisions possible given the circumstances and the information available. That said, occasions will come up when you make a wrong decision. You have two choices. You can either stubbornly stand by your decision regardless of the consequences or you can admit that the decision was not the right one and take action. The right choice is pretty clear.

Camcare's Phillip Goodwin and his board faced this choice. In the 1990s, much like other hospitals did, Camcare made the decision to build an integrated delivery system and, as part of its growth strategy, to purchase a HMO. The decision was predicated on the belief that the healthcare system was moving rapidly to becoming dominated by managed care and capitation. But in this particular market, unfortunately, growth projections were hugely overestimated. The HMO proved to be a tremendous financial drain on the system.

Board service isn't a popularity contest; it's a job—a tough job.

Despite differences of opinion on the board, the board decided to pull the plug on this unprofitable entity. "We recognized that the HMO had led to improvements in community health. But, ultimately, the board concluded that despite the positives, the HMO was bleeding the system dry. It was a hard decision, but it was an economically necessary decision," Goodwin said.

Clearly, had Goodwin's board refused to acknowledge that its assumptions going into the HMO purchases had been unrealistic and had it decided to keep the HMO in the system, the results could have proved ultimately disastrous, not only for the HMO and the system but potentially for the community.

The stakes were high on this one. But perhaps no higher than for many decisions your board will make. You have a responsibility to make decisions, to track them once they are executed, and to take corrective action when necessary. Admitting that you're wrong may not be without its costs; some people will likely say "I told you so." But, again, board service isn't a popularity contest; it's a job—a tough job.

THE COMMUNITY IS WATCHING

If you sit on the board of an investor-owned system, you may assume that this section doesn't apply to you. We disagree. Rural hospitals, large integrated delivery systems, hospitals that belong to religious orders, and those that are part of systems traded on a national exchange may be accountable to different bodies; but in the final analysis, they all serve communities and people.

The community will ultimately make or break you, no matter what. In the not-too-distant past, we witnessed one large investor-owned system lose sight of this fact and reap the consequences on Wall Street and in communities throughout the country.

The time-tested adage "do well by doing good" continues to be true very much today. If you fail the people your organization serves, your organization ultimately fails. If you make promises that you don't keep, your organization ultimately fails. If you put financial interests above human interests, your organization ultimately fails.

So why did Camcare decide to divest itself of the HMO when it clearly was serving the community's interests? In this case, Camcare appeared to be putting long-term community interests before short-term interests. In other words, because of the deleterious effect that the HMO was having on Camcare's financial viability, continuing to finance it would over time erode Camcare's ability to provide the community with the quality and access to care that it needs. Clearly, divesting the HMO created some ill will in the community and created somewhat of a public relations challenge; but over time, one hopes that Camcare will be able to demonstrate that it is very much committed to serving the community through its programs, services, and medical care.

Remaining community focused has never been more difficult for board members. They are struggling with issues related to federal statutes, such as the Balanced Budget Act, and compliance laws. They are grappling with issues borne out of organizational growth, including those related to mergers and acquisitions. They are dealing with explosions in new medical technology, which have the potential to revolutionize care but may carry a hefty price tag, and a concomitant information explosion that has raised a host of privacy issues. At any given board meeting, the board may face issues that heretofore it has never had to consider.

So how do you as a board member retain your community focus? Unfortunately, there is no one way and no right way. At a

If you fail the people your organization serves, your organization ultimately fails. If you make promises that you don't keep, your organization ultimately fails. If you put financial interests above human interests, your organization ultimately fails.

minimum, for each issue that confronts you and the entire board, you will want to ask "How will this affect the community?" and then take the time to answer it. You are responsible for answering this question *before* this decision is made, not in response to a community backlash. We also want to be clear on something else: This is not about putting a positive "spin" on decisions that clearly will meet with public resistance or criticism. Similarly, it does not mean always having to make decisions that will keep the community happy. Your job is to make decisions that will ensure that the organization your board serves remains financially sound, socially responsible, and always focused on doing right by those who are counting on you in sickness and in health.

That said, your board colleagues and CEO understand that if you are a new board member, you may be reluctant early on to take up the gauntlet on important issues. A number of our board chair interviewees said that they tended to be more observers than participants early in their board service. "When I looked at the make up of the board, I was intimidated. No question about it. It probably took me a good year-and-a-half to two years before I felt really comfortable speaking up, particularly when I had a dissenting opinion," recalled Brad Hansen, board chair of John C. Lincoln Health Network. The good news is that Hansen and the others we interviewed said that their reticence dissipated as they became more familiar with their organizations and their roles as board members.

We were struck by the simplicity and profundity of Yampa Valley's former CEO Margaret Sabin's take on what constitutes board effectiveness; she put it this way: "An effective board is one that can reach consensus and understand that even though some members of the board may disagree with the decision, that except for when they are in the room with the door shut, they will publicly absolutely support the overall board decision."

We could not have said it better ourselves.

Your job is to make decisions that will ensure that the organization your board serves remains financially sound, socially responsible, and always focused on doing right by those who are counting on you in sickness and in health.

BOARD COMPENSATION

Virtually all board members of investor-owned organizations are compensated for their board service. But should the same be true for not-for-profit board members? This is an issue that generates considerable debate, and one that is unlikely to have a "one-size-fits-all" answer.

Our observation is that organizations that do compensate their board members pay an amount that includes both a retainer and remuneration for each meeting that a member attends. Although very few, if any, board members may need the money, just knowing they are being compensated seems to raise their level of conscientiousness.

However, while studies and surveys have been conducted about the number of organizations that pay their board members, little has been written about the results achieved by paying organizations. According to the studies we have read, between 15 percent and 25 percent of the hospitals and systems in the United States compensate their board members. In addition, we have some anecdotal evidence that organizations that compensate their boards have a good experience recruiting new board members, have high attendance at board meetings, and have and can easily conduct self-assessment surveys.

We strongly believe that boards should at least discuss and review the concept of paying fees to their members. Generally, board members themselves will not raise the subject, so it should be raised by the chair or the CEO.

A number of authors have reviewed the pros and cons of compensating board members, including Dennis Pointer and Charlie Ewell and Jordan Hadelman and Jamie Orlikoff. Exhibits 4.1 and 4.2 present the main concepts of those writings.

Because different schools of thought battle on this issue, we do believe the issue of board member compensation deserves

We strongly
believe that
boards should at
least discuss
and review the
concept of paying
fees to their
members.

> **Exhibit 4.1: Why Board Members Should Be Paid**
>
> - Compensation, regardless of the actual amount paid, increases their attendance and participation at meetings. Also, paid members appear to do better preparation for meetings. Board members who don't want to be compensated can donate the money to the organization and receive a tax deduction.
> - Compensation sends a very clear message: The board's work is important; a board member's time is valuable not only at the board meetings but in preparation for those meetings; and the organization values the board's full attention and is willing to pay to achieve that. Most paid board chairs view compensation as a way to recognize board members' efforts, rather than as an incentive for better performance.
> - Compensation does not necessarily diminish the community-oriented and charitable mission of the hospital; rather, it may allow participation by community representatives who might not otherwise be able to afford to serve. This will broaden the composition of the board because members of disenfranchised populations will be able to afford to serve.
> - Compensation allows more flexibility in board member recruitment. A growing number of CEOs report having trouble recruiting qualified board members; this problem seems to have worsened in the past five years. An organization can be much more selective in recruiting if it can move outside its immediate community, and such members can bring an objective viewpoint to the job. More hospitals are adding one or two board members who are not part of the organization or immediate community. Recruiting such individuals, however, can be quite awkward if they are expected to pay their own expenses and not receive at least minimal compensation for participation in board activities.
> - Compensation diminishes feelings of "whatever we do is fine because we're only volunteers," which is prevalent in boards of not-for-profit organizations.

thorough review and discussion. Regardless of the outcome, the discussion can also be used as a lead-in for additional deliberations on topics such as the development of more effective leadership, commitment, and motivation at the board level.

Exhibit 4.2: Why Board Members Should Not Be Paid

- Compensation conflicts with a school of thought that submits that the very essence of voluntary trusteeship precludes compensation; volunteers get far greater satisfaction from their accomplishments and make a greater contribution because they serve for purely altruistic, rather than monetary, reasons.
- Compensation may worry board members that their receipt of payment for services they rendered will appear to be a conflict of interest.
- Compensation introduces an economic variable that may interfere with the board's ability to objectively conduct an honest and complete self-assessment program.
- Compensation causes fear among board members of losing their indemnification privileges as volunteer directors if they are compensated because state laws in this area are so vaguely written. Most statutes make clear that board members are expected to act in good faith within the scope of their official action and duties; but because they are so vague otherwise, any challenges will likely end up for the courts to decide.
- Compensation does not provide scientific evidence that it improves recruitment or performance of board members of not-for-profit organizations. Only anecdotal proof is available.
- Compensation, especially a small amount, may or may not make much difference in attracting and retaining the most qualified individuals.

As we emphasize throughout the book, we believe that serving effectively on the board of a hospital or healthcare system requires that individuals have knowledge of the industry, knowledge of the difference between governance and management, and experience serving on other governing boards. The hospital or healthcare system is in many instances the largest corporation in a community, has the most employees, and the largest revenue base, which require the most talented board members available. These organizations may likely consider board compensation as much a financial investment in their future success as the compensation packages paid to their full-time executive management team.

5

Board Member Selection
and Composition

ARE EFFECTIVE BOARDS the result of good fortune or are they the result of careful selection of board members? We would argue for the latter. That said, who should be involved in the identification and ultimate selection of board members? Our research suggested that the responsibility is the joint effort of the CEO, the board chair, and the current board. (Even if board members are government appointed—as is the case with boards of municipal hospitals—CEOs can and should play a central role in identifying future board members.)

CEOs can and should play a central role in identifying future board members.

Hospitals and systems throughout the country use a number of different approaches to identify future board members. We discuss some of those approaches in this chapter, from the most risky attempts to the safest bets.

FACTORS TO CONSIDER IN BOARD SELECTION

Community Stature

Particularly in small towns where everybody knows everybody, the tendency is to select community leaders to serve on the board. The choice may be the school board president, bank president, or owner of a large business. If you are lucky, choosing someone whom the community knows and respects will translate into effective board service. But don't take it as a given.

The board must not be a place for people to "practice" board service.

Unless this community leader had a former life as a healthcare executive, community standing is likely to have only a minimal bearing on his or her performance on the board. Having this individual on the board may look good, but when the board gets down to work, this individual is likely to be as effective or ineffective as any other board member.

Volunteer Experience

People volunteer for board service for a variety of reasons. For some, it's a sincere desire to give back to the community, while for others it's an opportunity for self-aggrandizement. We are not suggesting that you should second-guess the motives of someone who volunteers for board service, but neither should you jump at the opportunity to accept anyone who volunteers. Do some homework and learn more about this individual, beginning with a face-to-face discussion. Take time to learn about the individual's past volunteer experience including type, location, duration, and demonstrated level of commitment. In other words, the board must not be a place for people to "practice" board service. Ideally, they should have already "practiced" elsewhere. Certainly, you shouldn't go on this fact-finding mission without letting the prospective board member know that it is your responsibility to gather such information. We believe that anyone who wants to join the board for the right reasons will understand that you cannot be cavalier in identifying future board members. If you meet with resistance, this may indeed be a red flag.

Recommendation

Word of mouth is a common way of identifying future board members. We argue, however, that absent some checks-and-balances, it is a risky method. At best, recommendations are only a first step. In other words, if you respect the individual who made the recommendation, then the referred individual should be taken seriously. But as is the case with the volunteers for board service, the recommended candidate must demonstrate that he or she is "right" for the job by virtue of your mutual discussion and based on past successful volunteer experience.

Past Board Membership

Many organizations have term limits and have put constraints on the number of consecutive terms allowed. As a result, some board members must rotate off the board for a year or so before they are eligible to rejoin the board. (See the end of this chapter for our thoughts on term limits.) Should you jump at the chance to return such a member to the board upon expiration of the waiting period? Maybe, but maybe not. If the individual was a dynamic and effective board member, you might think that bringing him or her back is a "no-risk" situation. In fact, that may be true. But keep in mind that the healthcare marketplace changes at lightning speed. The issues that were relevant yesterday may be nonissues today. As a result, you can't assume that the past board member will hit the ground running on the new board. Worse yet, this individual may be tied to the way things were done last time around and may be surprisingly resistant to the current way the board conducts business, particularly if the board chair has changed in the interim.

Perhaps just as important is the fact that by bringing back a prior board member, you are limiting opportunities for new, valuable additions to your board. Although something can be said for continuity on the board, just as much can be said for adding a fresh perspective. You must carefully weigh the pros and cons of bringing a board member back. Saying "no, thank you" may not be easy, but may be the right thing to do for the board and the organization.

Service in Another Volunteer Capacity

The surest way to identify a first-rate board member is by identifying "superstars" who have been volunteering at the organization in other capacities. Subsidiary boards, foundation boards, hospital committees, and issue-specific task forces all require the services of volunteers. These boards and committees provide a wonderful training ground for future board members and provide you with an opportunity to see who is up to the challenge and who is not.

Almost without exception, the board chairs we interviewed said that they began serving their organizations through some voluntary role in another capacity. Similarly, virtually every CEO we interviewed heartily endorsed the practice of observing prospective board members in action in these other roles. They agreed that perhaps no better way than this exists to evaluate an individual's commitment and effectiveness. John Cramer, president and CEO of PinnacleHealth System, said: "I try to keep my antenna up as to who might make good board members by bringing them into the organization to serve on the foundation board. If you're on the foundation board, you gain a good understanding of the system, its goals, its values, and strategic plan, and yet you don't have a lot of responsibility. The other thing I do is to make sure that each committee has one or two volunteers on it. This way we are able to take a lot of the guesswork out of board member selection."

We cannot overemphasize the importance of the board selection process to the ongoing effectiveness of the board. Many boards allow members to serve two three-year terms. Six years can seem like an eternity when you have a board member who clearly is the wrong fit. We are not suggesting that you should ignore an individual's community stature or another individual's recommendation. Rather, you should develop a pipeline for

Exhibit 5.1: Questions for Board Chair Selection

- Does this individual demonstrate a good understanding of the organization and its long-term needs?
- Does this individual understand the board's role as policy-maker?
- Does this individual come to meetings prepared?
- Does this individual make valuable contributions—that is, does he or she raise pertinent questions and provide valuable insights?
- Is this individual respected by his or her board colleagues?
- Is this individual a good listener who considers others' perspectives before making decisions?
- Does this individual have the ability to draw out others who might otherwise be apt to remain silent?
- Does this individual seem to understand the balance between discussing an issue fully and reaching decisions in a timely fashion?

prospective board members that begins with their service in another volunteer position for your organization.

BOARD CHAIR SELECTION

Just as you can evaluate potential board members who are fit for the board through observing their contributions and style as they serve your organization in another volunteer capacity, you can evaluate which of your board members have the potential for solid performance as a board chair by observing them during the course of their board service. In our opinion, the selection of board chairs is second only in importance to CEO selection. Exhibit 5.1 lists questions you need to ask when evaluating a potential board chair.

If your answer is "yes" to these questions, then the individual being considered as a board chair is apt to be a good choice. We must note, however, that several CEOs we interviewed said that some board members appeared to undergo "personality transformations" when they became chairs.

Unfortunately, such transformations do occur and are often unpredictable. In such cases, CEOs and boards have little recourse. Although the CEO or a board member can certainly take the board chair aside and tactfully point out that certain behaviors are compromising the board's effectiveness, realistically such conversations are potentially damaging to the CEO's career.

BOARD COMPOSITION

So far, our focus has been on identifying individuals who have the right combination of organizational knowledge and people skills to serve the organization effectively. But board member selection must also be viewed in a larger context—that is, whether the individuals chosen to serve collectively represent the right mix. In other words, is the whole greater than the sum of the parts?

To some extent, the composition of the board will be a function of board size. The larger the board, the more diverse it is likely to be. That said, we are not suggesting that large boards— say, upwards of 15—are the answer, but quite the contrary. Our interviews reinforced our belief that smaller boards tend to be more efficient and effective. As a general rule, consider that:

- most effective boards have between 10 and 15 members; and
- boards vary in effectiveness when they have 16 to 25 members.

We have yet to see a truly effective board with more than 25 members.

Unfortunately, many organizations fall victim to "board size creep" in today's healthcare world because of the trend toward mergers and acquisitions. Merging existing governance bodies becomes part of the deal, not because anyone believes that it will enhance the governance function, but because it is the politically correct thing to do.

In fact, a 1997 survey of hospital and health system governance conducted jointly by the American Hospital Association's Center for Health Care Leadership and Ernst & Young LLP found that 25 percent of hospital boards and 39 percent of system boards had 16 or more voting board members. Such boards may satisfy political interests. Our interviewees confirmed, however, that these large boards do little to satisfy organizational interests largely because at least a handful of these board members never get the chance to voice an opinion—because either there isn't enough time to hear from everyone or everyone gets a chance to voice an opinion and time runs out before decisions can be made.

> **Large boards do little to satisfy organizational interests largely because at least a handful of these board members never get the chance to voice an opinion.**

We have heard the argument that system boards should be smaller than hospital boards because they should be addressing only "big-picture" strategy issues. We have also heard that system boards should be larger than hospital boards because of the complexity of the organization they govern. We believe that this is actually not a worthwhile comparison; the important consideration is the size of the board as it relates to the organization's needs. In other words, you do not simply want to say "This is the size our board has always been, so it must be fine" or "Our board size is governed by our bylaws, so it isn't open for discussion." Changing the status quo or revising bylaws may take some work; but difficult as it is, it may, in some cases, be well advised.

Look periodically at the size of your board. Involve the board in an honest, open discussion about whether the board has become too insular (so small that groupthink frequently occurs) or too expansive ("like an AHA Convention," as one CEO put it) to be efficient and effective. If your discussion suggests that the board needs to be "resized," then by all means do so.

The size of the board is one variable that affects its composition. Obviously, the larger the board, the more opportunities to infuse it with diversity. Beyond that, board composition is a factor either of legal dictates (in the case of a municipal hospital), organizational policies, or historical expectations about who should serve on the board. For the most part, our CEO interviewees said that board composition is not mandated but is a function of historical expectations—the most common being that the board has strong community representation. Certainly, another common expectation that has gained momentum over the past decade is that boards have physician representation.

One CEO we spoke to, however, approaches board composition somewhat differently. Philip Newbold, president and CEO of Memorial Health System, strives for a balance on his system board, which has 13 members. "We try to make sure our board has balance across three areas," Newbold said. "You find that about a third of your board really like community involvement, and they are there to reflect community values and diversity. Then, there's another third that like strategy—physician integration, diversification issues, etc. Then there's another third that like the numbers. From what I have observed, these three groups tend to always be there and should be there. If you get too many people who focus on finances, then every decision becomes financially driven. If you get too many people in strategy, then you run the risk of growing too fast and maybe things don't work out as intended. Similarly, if the board is only focused on the community, then tough, but necessary, business decisions may not be made. Sure, when your board members represent three very different orientations, there will be creative tension from time to time, but that's a good thing."

We have to admit that Newbold's approach to board composition appeals to us. It is not precise nor is it likely to be foolproof, but it does seem to be worth serious consideration. The notion of balance is one we cannot overemphasize. Lopsided boards make lopsided decisions.

Another CEO who spends a great deal of time and effort to identify prospective board members is Peter Bastone, president and CEO of Mission Hospital Regional Medical Center in Mission Viejo, California. Since becoming the hospital's CEO, Bastone has formed what is called a "CEO Advisory." The Advisory comprises about 80 individuals from area businesses. "The group meets twice a year, and usually about 30 people show up, and we talk to them about their companies' healthcare-related issues like workers' comp, the cost of pharmaceuticals, etc.," Bastone explained. "These meetings get the group interested in what the hospital is doing and how we do it, but the meetings also give me a chance to see who might be good additions to our board. So far, I've drawn two board members from the Advisory — a president of a local car dealership and the superintendent of schools."

"OUTSIDE" BOARD MEMBERS

For obvious reasons, corporate America values board members who bring a blend of perspective and talent. As a result, businesses in other sectors go virtually anywhere in the country to find such individuals. Investor-owned hospital systems often do the same. But when you raise the subject of recruiting board members who are not from within the community or industry, you typically elicit strong opinions both for and against the idea.

In our opinion, boards of not-for-profit healthcare organizations should not restrict board service to individuals from the community. Although we believe the community should be strongly represented on the board, at least one or two board members could come from "outside" and could greatly enhance board effectiveness.

Why do we take this position? First, because healthcare is a complex business, it can benefit from the business acumen of leaders from other industries. For example, executives who are intimately involved in working with bond-rating agencies can be a valuable advisor to a healthcare board planning to undertake a sizeable bond issue.

Because health-care is a complex business, it can benefit from the business acumen of leaders from other industries.

Second, healthcare organizations and their boards can unwittingly become insular—mired in their own problems and reliant on tried-and-true solutions. Outside board members can add a fresh perspective on the situation and often propose solutions the board might otherwise not consider.

Outside board members can add a fresh perspective on the situation and often propose solutions the board might otherwise not consider.

We must add a note of caution, however. The addition of outside board members is only a good thing if the individuals invited to serve are carefully identified and evaluated based on solid criteria. Outside board members, just like local board members, must be willing, able, and selected to serve for the right reasons.

CROSS-GENERATIONAL BOARDS

In times past, board service was generally reserved for senior careerists—individuals who were 50 or older and with an impressive list of accomplishments on résumés that do not fit on a single page. Today, an increasing number of organizations are recognizing the value of adding board members who may not be as far along in their careers but who can infuse new life and vibrancy into board deliberations. We applaud this recognition, but we believe that recognizing the value of younger board members in and of itself is not enough.

When you have multiple generations serving on a board, a generation gap of sorts is likely to be present. Failure to close the gap can severely compromise board effectiveness. Exhibit 5.2 lists tips, adapted from the National Center for Nonprofit Boards, for bridging the generation gap on boards.

Diversity in terms of business expertise seems to be a given on most healthcare boards. Yet diversity in terms of age, ethnicity, and gender is still a work in progress. But based on our interviews, we are pleased to report that things are changing, albeit slowly. Almost without exception the CEOs we talked with said that their boards and board nominating committees are acutely aware of the need to bring more diversity into the boardroom and are working toward that end.

Diversity in terms of age, ethnicity, and gender is still a work in progress.

TERM LIMITS

Two schools of thought exist about term limits. Those in favor of term limits argue that these limits ensure that the board has a continuous infusion of fresh thinking. They also argue that term limits safeguard the board against being stuck with a contentious or ineffective board member for years on end. We understand the logic here, but we disagree.

We do not believe that term limits are necessary for board members, particularly if your organization has practiced due diligence in its board member selection process, provided good orientation for new members, and conducted annual board self-assessments. Term limits can actually work to your disadvantage for a simple reason: Healthcare governance is not an easy skill to learn, and your organization and the industry in which it operates are extremely complex. A policy of systematically rotating members off the board will deprive your board of the benefits of your experienced members.

We are not suggesting that you just bide time until an ineffective board member who has become an obstacle decides to step down. In such cases, we believe the board chair has the duty to privately suggest to the ineffective board member not to seek reelection. Clearly, such a suggestion is more effective when concrete examples of how the board member has fallen short of

Exhibit 5.2: Seven Tips for Bridging the Generation Gap on Boards

1. Encourage board members to get to know each other. Every agenda should provide time for board members to share what is going on in their lives since the last meeting.
2. Examine stereotypes. Don't assume that younger board members have the "life experiences" necessary to contribute meaningfully in the boardroom. This, of course, is a gross generalization. Further, boards can have myopic vision and not consider the contributions that younger board members can make over time. The article notes that boards would be wise to recruit a "promising baby boomer now who will have more influence and assets later."
3. Consider mentoring. The mentoring process can be valuable not just for younger board members but for all new board members. By pairing the newcomer with a veteran board member, the newer member doesn't have the feeling of "I'm in this alone."
4. Ensure that all members participate in meetings. The article asserts that "the board chair should ensure that all generations participate in board decisions and that a few outspoken board members do not monopolize the debate."
5. Avoid tokenism. A single, younger board member is bound to get labeled as just that. If you can avoid this situation, the tendency toward tokenism will be minimized.
6. Consider training. Younger members of your board may welcome additional guidance beyond that offered in the board orientation. While you do not want to single them out for special training, you should be prepared to provide them with additional guidance or training if they request it.
7. Cultivate an ongoing matchmaking process. The article recommends that not-for-profits undergo an ongoing matchmaking process to identify young leaders and develop a pool of talented people who are potential board members. They must also be able to demonstrate that their organizations are relevant to the interests of the younger generation; this includes their willingness to address issues of concern to younger adults.

Source: Adapted from The National Center for Nonprofit Boards. Washington, D.C.

expectations—sporadic attendance at meetings, repeated non-productive clashes with the rest of the board, and so on—are given.

If you are skeptical about abandoning term limits, we offer another option: reelection of board members annually or every other year. This provides you with a measure of control over the situation without mandating that certain, valuable board members step down at a specific point in time.

Although we do not advocate term limits for board members, we do support term limits for board chairs. Specifically, we recommend electing the chair for either two two-year terms or one five-year term. We also strongly suggest that the chair first serve as chair-elect, giving him or her the opportunity to closely observe the roles and responsibilities of the chair.

6

Physician Representation on the Board

HEALTHCARE ORGANIZATION BOARDS without physician members have become the exception to the rule. In fact, for a quarter of the board to be made up of physicians is not uncommon. The survey by the AHA and Ernst & Young LLP, cited in Chapter 5, found that 81 percent of hospital respondents and 72 percent of system respondents had voting physician members on their board; roughly a third of both groups had at least three voting physician members.

But we did interview several CEOs who do not have physicians on their boards and do not believe that lack of physician representation on the boards hurts their organizations in any way. Instead, they maintained that having an effective conduit in place between the board and the medical staff is important to ensure that medical staff and patient care issues reach the boardroom and are addressed appropriately. One hospital CEO said that although the chiefs of staff of his system's four hospitals are not voting board members, they attend every board meeting to report on quality and credentialing as well as provide insights and perspectives on issues that affect the medical staff.

Although this practice appears to work well for this organization, we are among those who believe that, ideally, physicians should be voting members of the board. When you consider the tremendous influence of the medical staff on perceptions of the organization; the quality of care delivered; and, ultimately, the bottom line, having physicians on the board seems a clear necessity. That said, identifying the right physicians to serve on the board and integrating them onto the board are no small feats.

Although many organizations systematically appoint their chiefs of staff to the board, in part as a nod to political correctness, this practice is not necessarily effective. If politics compels you to appoint the chief of staff, but you realize that this individual may not fill the bill entirely, we encourage you to appoint yet another physician to the board using the same rigorous standards for selection that you use with other board member appointments.

Ideally, physicians should be voting members of the board.

Dan Coleman, president and CEO of John C. Lincoln Health Network, put it this way: "I have found that the effectiveness of physicians on the board varies tremendously. There are some physicians who can really look at things in the broad context and then there are those who can tend to be myopic—to the point where they aren't even representing the medical staff but their own practices."

If you are wondering whether the appropriate role for physician board members is to wear their medical staff hats or to attempt to put their natural allegiance to the medical staff aside, the answer is both. Obviously, one reason you have physicians on the board is to provide representation for the medical staff. At the same time, situations occur when keeping the medical staff happy does not necessarily serve the long-term interests of the organization.

One CEO we interviewed found that the best way to ensure that physicians on the board don't always, or never, advocate for the medical staff is to increase the number of physicians at the board table. One-third of the board at Hays Medical Center comprises physicians. With the exception of the hospital's president of medical staff, who is one of these board members, the physicians have been told: "You guys have to wear the hat of the organization; you have to," explained John Jeter, M.D., the hospital's president and CEO. "On the other hand, we've told the president of the medical staff that he must wear the hat of the medical staff. I know this approach may be controversial, but my feeling is the chief of staff must represent the medical staff. So if everyone else votes 'yea' on an issue and the chief of staff votes 'nay' because that vote is in the medical staff's interest, he can at least go back to the medical staff and tell them he voted the way they wanted him to vote."

Interestingly, according to Jeter, the chief of staff voted against the majority only one time in recent history. This suggests, he contended, that the polarization between physicians and other board members is more a concern in theory than in reality.

We agree with Jeter's approach. The president of the medical staff should indeed represent the medical staff's interests. By virtue of his or her position, this individual probably should serve as an ex officio member of the board. We also agree with Jeter that other physician board members are on the board to represent the best interests of the organization as a whole.

Of course, some people would disagree. One CEO we interviewed said his physician board members seem to be absolutely incapable of seeing the big picture. The result, he said, is that the other board members almost routinely discount what these physicians have to say.

Clearly, if board members dismiss the views of physicians who sit on the board, the purpose of having physician board members is clearly defeated. So how do you ensure that physicians are respected and valued as board members? This may sound simplistic, but first you have to believe that they have something to offer.

No one disputes the fact that physicians are highly educated and that typically they are highly motivated individuals. However, many believe that physicians are solely motivated by two things: (1) a desire to make decisions independently and (2) a desire to do so at financial gain. Certainly, some physicians do fall into that category and, certainly, some physicians who sit on boards do reinforce that stereotype. However, many more physician board members do see the big picture and want to make a valuable contribution to the governance of their organizations.

Physicians' ability to be valuable contributors will depend on a number of factors including, as noted above, being given the opportunity to do so. Physicians should be given meaningful committee assignments just as the other board members are given them. Also, physicians should be included in all activities designed to orient and educate the board. In other words, just because they practice, or have practiced, medicine at the organization doesn't mean that they understand the inner workings of the organization or its governance challenges.

You should also embrace the unique perspective that physicians bring. Although you want them to see the big picture, they do possess a wealth of knowledge and insight about a key constituency—the medical staff, who has the ability to make or break your organization. When your physician board members voice medical staff concerns, listen—and listen carefully. These physician members serve as an "early warning system" of trouble that may be afoot, and they can help you avoid contentious situations down the road. They also hear patient concerns but are vigilant for conflict-of-interest issues.

Clearly, identifying physicians to serve on the board may be more art than science. That said, we think that some guidelines may be helpful. First, let's consider physicians who are not appropriate for board service.

We do not believe that hospital-based physicians should serve on the board. This group generally includes pathologists, radiologists, anesthesiologists, hospitalists, intensivists, medical directors, emergency room physicians, or any physician who is on the hospital payroll or who has a contract with the hospital. Why? For example, the hospital CEO will find difficulty in not recommending the purchase of a particular piece of equipment for radiology if the staff radiologist is a member of the board or, worse yet, is the board chair or a board officer. Likewise, if an

Physicians should be given meaningful committee assignments just as the other board members are given them.

When your physician board members voice medical staff concerns, listen—and listen carefully.

anesthesiologist comes to the CEO and wants his or her group to have an "exclusive contract" with the hospital but doesn't want the group to be prevented from providing anesthesiologist services to a competing surgery center, the anesthesiologist on the board will find difficulty in considering this issue objectively.

Besides physicians who may have conflict of interest by virtue of their hospital-based status, we believe that another physician candidate type should not be selected—the squeaky wheel. Some boards tend to put vocal physician critics on the board in the hope that such a move will quiet the dissenter. This sounds good in theory, but unfortunately it rarely works as planned. We are not suggesting that you avoid putting physicians with strong opinions on the board, but quite the contrary. Your board is strengthened by strong opinionated members, so long as those individuals have no particular axe to grind or are not obstructionists by nature. As we all know, heavy-handed behavior rarely produces good results and can very well derail an otherwise productive board.

So which physicians should seriously be considered for board service? Before we offer our thoughts, we want to make another important point: Do not ask the medical staff for recommendations. The medical staff should be represented at board meetings by the medical staff president. The board, through its nominating committee, should be charged with identifying other physicians for board service. This methodical process should be much the same as that used to identify nonphysician board members. Briefly, here are criteria that should be considered:

Experience

Physicians who lack other board experience should not be selected. You can often determine who has previous board experience and who does not from the physicians' résumés, which should be on file at the hospital and relatively current given that all medical staff members have to be reappointed on a regular basis.

We do not believe that hospital-based physicians should serve on the board.

Some boards tend to put vocal physician critics on the board in the hope that such a move will quiet the dissenter. This sounds good in theory, but unfortunately it rarely works as planned.

The medical staff should be represented at board meetings by the medical staff president. The board, through its nominating committee, should be charged with identifying other physicians for board service.

Achievement

Physicians' résumés should also provide information about their achievements. Have they been elected to offices by local, state, or national medical societies or other groups? Have they received other types of awards from their peers? Have they achieved something or been recognized for an activity outside of medicine? Do they possess the kinds of knowledge or achievement experiences that would benefit the board?

Management Skills

Résumés may also be reviewed to determine if a physician has done anything to enhance his or her management skills. What kind of nonclinical continuing education has the physician pursued in the past five years? Many physicians today are completing MBAs or attending short-term management courses sponsored by professional associations or universities. Is the physician the managing partner of a group practice? To maintain their present income levels in today's turbulent environment, physicians need creativity and skills in management, financial knowledge, and the management of people.

Ability To Be A Team Player

Governance is a team sport. The board's nominating committee should look for indications that a physician is, or could be, a team player. Some clinical specialties tend to emphasize teamwork more than others. Most physicians, however, are not trained to be team players. A physician who has been highly autonomous for a number of years may have trouble adapting to the idea that he or she is just one of many players in the boardroom.

Personal Qualities

Some of the qualities that should be considered are intelligence, which is probably a given in most cases; compassion; common sense; and a willingness to be a good listener. Certainly, the physician must also demonstrate high moral and ethical standards. Integrity is a must.

Objectivity

You must identify physicians who you believe are capable of and willing to come to board meetings with open minds and no personal agendas. They must be committed to putting the organization's welfare first in all deliberations.

Receptivity to Training and Education

Physicians understand the value of ongoing clinical education. The same physicians may be less receptive to training to improve their governance skills, however. We spoke with one CEO who admitted that he has "given up" on trying to get his new physician board members to participate in the hospital's board-orientation program. He said they absolutely refuse to attend. Before you appoint a physician to your board, you need to make participation in board orientation and other board education a condition of board service. If the physician says "no," we suggest that you continue your search for the board position.

Special Considerations

Boards of smaller hospitals in rural communities have a particularly difficult challenge in identifying physicians for board service because few physicians serve on the medical staff. If a hospital

> You must identify physicians who you believe are capable of and willing to come to board meetings with open minds and no personal agendas.

> Before you appoint a physician to your board, you need to make participation in board orientation and other board education a condition of board service.

has nine physicians who live in the community, serve on the medical staff, and belong to two different practice groups, selecting one of them to serve in addition to the president of the medical staff can be potentially difficult. Selecting a physician from the same group that the medical staff president belongs to can leave the board open to charges of favoritism. Selecting a physician from the competing group, on the other hand, might result in a lack of cooperation on certain issues. In such cases, your nominating committee may wish to consider inviting a (non-competing) physician from a neighboring community to sit on the board.

County and district hospitals also are often challenged to get physicians on the board. These hospitals' board members typically are elected or are political appointments. Encouraging otherwise busy physicians to run for election or to court a political appointment is often difficult.

In such cases, a board that desires physician input will essentially have to mount its own "political campaign" either to convince qualified physicians to throw their hat in the ring or to convince the county commissioners (or other group charged with appointing board members) to appoint physicians with the needed expertise.

Clearly, the road to identifying board-compatible physicians and integrating them effectively into governance activities remains a bumpy one. Some organizations seem to have more success than others. If you are among those organizations that still have some work to do in this regard, our advice is simple: keep trying. Ultimately, the board and the organization will benefit from your efforts.

7

Board and Committee Structure

IN THIS CHAPTER, we discuss the issue of board and committee structures. As noted in Chapter 5, a hospital and health system governance survey by the AHA and Ernst & Young LLP found that 25 percent of hospital boards and 39 percent of system boards had 16 or more voting board members. In the same chapter, we also argued that a "right" board size is difficult to ascertain. We are convinced, however, that some indicators can signal if your board is too large, including:

- you routinely fail to reach decisions at board meetings because too many people must be heard before decisions are reached;
- you have to stretch to make meaningful committee assignments for all board members;
- you don't notice when a particular board member is missing at a meeting; and
- you can't comfortably fit all the needed chairs around the meeting table. This is said partly in jest, but it is not far from the truth in some organizations.

THE SYSTEMS' STRUGGLE

Perhaps the organizations that struggle the most with board size are healthcare systems, many of which have been created through the merger of several organizations. For integrated systems, the challenge of structuring the system board is fraught with political landmines. Mergers are inherently sensitive undertakings and care must be taken not to disenfranchise those who have been loyal volunteers over time. The good news is that although building an effective board may take time, doing so is indeed possible. Consider the following two situations:

Although building an effective board may take time, doing so is indeed possible.

Situation A

When Knox Singleton, president and CEO of INOVA Health System, served as executive vice president in 1983, the system had one board with 30 members and 33 different operating units. The board was a reflection of INOVA's growth in the 1970s and '80s from a one-hospital entity to a four-hospital system with a complement of other healthcare services. In the 1980s, INOVA changed its governance structure so that it had a parent board and operating boards for each of its four hospitals, as well as separate boards for its alternate care, continuing care, nursing home, urgent care, and other adjunct operating units.

"At the height of our decentralized board structure, we had 13 different boards. We created a classic Tower of Babel," Singleton explained. "In one sense, it was terrific because we had a lot of people from the community involved in the governance process. The problem was that there was only 'real' work for about a dozen or so, and the rest didn't really have much to do. There was a second issue. We had a couple of circumstances where a particular issue would be handled several times by different boards, and each of which reached a different conclusion. Everyone began asking, 'Who's in charge here?'"

By the early 1990s, Singleton and the vast majority of INOVA's boards realized that the governance process needed to be streamlined. "Today, we have what we call a holographic governance system. You can cut it up and really divide issues between what today are two boards," Singleton said. "Quality issues, community issues, and system integration are all the purview of the healthcare services board. Issues related to strategic planning, budget development, capital structure remain under the purview of the parent board. So everybody handles an issue only once, and the decision of the one board is the final decision. Both boards now have authority, accountability, and there is a lot less wasted time."*

Situation B

John Cramer, president and CEO of PinnacleHealth System, has also grappled with the issue of system governance. PinnacleHealth was formed in January 1996 through the merger of the two largest and most competitive healthcare providers in Harrisburg, Pennsylvania. Following this merger, the newly formed PinnacleHealth merged again with a smaller osteopathic hospital. The end result is a system with 55 sites (outpatient clinics), a large home care system, hospital program, behavioral health units, and other entities to complete the continuum of care.

Initially, when PinnacleHealth and the osteopathic hospital consolidated, two main boards—a system board and a hospital board—provided governance. A third board, however, oversaw the system's physician joint ventures and primary care practices. "I had no illusions that it was going to work; it was politics," Cramer said. "Part of the merger agreement was that besides me, eight board members would come from one organization and eight from the other to form the new system board. But from day

---

*INOVA has a separate board that governs its foundation.

one, there was disagreement about what authority the system board had and what authority the hospital board had."

The solution, according to Cramer, was to make the two boards one and the same. In other words, the system board is also the hospital board. "We conduct a system board meeting, and we adjourn that. Then, we conduct a hospital board meeting, and we adjourn that," explained Cramer. Although several auxiliary boards still exist, such as the foundation and medical services boards, policy decisions at PinnacleHealth today are by and large the responsibility of a single, 22-person board. Cramer's goal is to reduce the board to 15 or 16 members over the next few years.

Cramer was the first to admit that the process of restructuring the governance team wasn't easy and most certainly wasn't always pleasant. He said that as CEO of the system, he always felt a responsibility to initiate the needed changes: "I needed to be the one to get the boards to understand why the current structure wasn't working. The issue then became the focus for more than one board retreat. We provided a lot of data, encouraged open discussion, and tried to work through the issues with the assistance of an independent facilitator. Beyond that, I worked hard to develop good relationships with individual board members, gain their trust, and plant the seeds for change."

INOVA's Singleton and PinnacleHealth's Cramer, CEOs of expansive systems, reached different conclusions about the "right" governance structure for their organizations, but agreed on a common element. They both opted for a simplified governance structure—simplified in terms of how decisions are made and where the accountability for decisions rests. Whether your organization is a single hospital or a complex system, practical governance is the ultimate goal. Your board or boards must be structured to facilitate efficient, informed decision making with clear lines of accountability. If you can relate to Singleton's experience of having multiple boards discuss and decide on a single issue, then now is the time to revisit your governance structure.

The process of restructuring the governance team isn't easy and most certainly isn't always pleasant.

Your board or boards must be structured to facilitate efficient, informed decision making with clear lines of accountability.

EXECUTIVE COMMITTEE OF THE BOARD

The role of the executive committee has not changed drastically over time. The committee—typically made up of board officers and, in some cases, chairs of standing committees—serves in three primary capacities: (1) emergency decision making, (2) streamlining the decision making process for the rest of the board, and (3) always evaluating the performance of the CEO. According to the survey by the AHA and Ernst & Young LLP, 45 percent of board chairs said their executive committees "only make emergency decisions," and 22 percent said their boards "streamline decisions." A smaller percentage—16 percent—said their executive committees make most decisions, and even fewer—8 percent—said their executive committees act as sounding boards for the CEO.

The frequency with which the executive committee meets varies depending on the size of the board and the complexity of its issues. Some executive committees meet regularly between scheduled board meetings, others meet quarterly, and still others meet only on an as-needed basis. Regardless of the frequency of the committee's meetings, any decisions made by the executive committee should be reported to the entire board at its next meeting.

In our view, the role of the executive committee appears to be what it should be. We would, however, like to see more of these committees involved in streamlining decisions for the rest of the board. In fact, streamlining decisions should be a primary function of all board committees.

BOARD COMMITTEES AND SUBCOMMITTEES

In our view, the work of board committees and subcommittees should be as important as the work of the full board. In theory—and in reality, in a growing number of organizations—these two

Regardless of the frequency of the committee's meetings, any decisions made by the executive committee should be reported to the entire board at its next meeting.

Streamlining decisions should be a primary function of all board committees.

Committees enable an organization to take complex issues or tasks and break them down into manageable projects.

> **Key Determinants of an Effective Committee or Subcommittee**
>
> - The committee has a clearly defined, written scope of responsibility.
> - The committee chair understands the committee's charge and is process-and-outcome oriented.
> - Committees have both board and staff representation, albeit minimal staff representation, except on finance; audit; and like committees, which typically require a greater number of staff or, at least, more senior staff.
> - Committee meetings are held based on necessity, rather than out of habit.
> - The committee has a defined process for addressing issues, reporting out to the full board, and recommending action.
> - Committees are disbanded if they have no real work to do.

groups can accomplish much of the groundwork for effective decision making by the full board.

Typically, board committees, besides the executive committee, include a finance/budget committee; nominating committee; strategic planning committee; and often compensation, audit, and quality assurance (clinical) committees. In some organizations, committees for such areas as ethics, professional affairs, and government relations, to name a few, also exist. Subcommittees may include smaller offshoots of the above, such as a capital project subcommittee.

When committees and subcommittees are structured properly and have serious work to attend to, the payoff is tremendous. First, it makes the committee members feel that they are making real contributions to the organization, more so than they are at times able to contribute by attending board meetings. Second, committees enable an organization to take complex issues or tasks and break them down into manageable projects. Third, the board and the organization have the reassurance that an issue was discussed thoroughly and not compromised by being one of a dozen items the board had to address at its meeting.

Consider what can—or cannot—happen when issues are not referred to a committee. Fred Wolf, immediate past chair at Steamboat Springs Health Care Association, said he lived through such an experience: "Under the previous board chairman's term, we floated a $30 million bond issue. It involved about ten discussions with the board. We appointed a project manager, and he would report for five or ten minutes at each board meeting. I said, 'Wait a minute. From my standpoint, these are really major issues that need to be addressed by an active finance committee and active construction committee. Five minutes at a board meeting doesn't cut it.' As board chairman, I was pretty vigilant by involving committees as needed. It worked for the board and it worked for the committees."

Many boards do try to use committees and subcommittees effectively, but the process breaks down as the group struggles with the best way to address specific issues. Typically the process is ad hoc, with one committee taking one approach and another committee another approach. Committees and subcommittees can be more efficient and productive if they adopt a standard operating procedure that results in the development of "issue briefings" for presentation to the full board (in the case of a committee) or to the committee (in the case of the subcommittee).

ISSUE BRIEFINGS

Issue briefings are similar to executive summaries in that they provide a capsule view of the issue, relevant background information, key questions that have been or need to be answered, options for addressing the issue, and the committee's or subcommittee's recommended action. Background information presented should be objective and not editorial in nature. (See Appendix E for a sample issue briefing.)

Quite simply, an issue briefing brings the full board up to speed quickly on the current issues. It jump starts the discussion

Committees and subcommittees can be more efficient and productive if they adopt a standard operating procedure that results in the development of "issue briefings."

because the full board, or committee, has the background information compiled by the committee or subcommittee and does not need to start at square one.

Issue briefings can profoundly change the board meeting process. If you are currently a board member, you probably know first hand that committee reports to the board can be tedious and largely unproductive. Rarely do you sit there poised for action. Instead, you peer at your agenda, wondering how long each committee report will last so that you can get down to the "real work." With issue briefings, committee reports are action oriented and are part of the "real work."

BOARD-CONVENED TASK FORCES

Board-convened task forces should be reserved for a single purpose—to address specific issues that can be resolved through discussions. In other words, these task forces should be convened with very specific charges and disbanded when their work is done. The types of issues that might be appropriate for task force consideration include a public-relations crisis, consideration of a particular capital-intensive purchase, a specific medical staff issue, and other particularly time-sensitive concerns.

The task force's job is to do the legwork to get to the heart of the issue and get answers quickly. Unlike committees, which may have the luxury of meeting monthly or every other month, the task force's work tends to be more immediate—work begins and concludes within a month or two. Also, task forces often benefit from staff representation because of the organizational knowledge these individuals can bring to the board.

8

Ethics Check

ASK ANY CEO how he or she protects against ethical breaches in the boardroom, and he or she is likely to point to his or her board's conflict-of-interest statement. These statements, which are rarely more than a page long and signed to indicate compliance by all board members, require board members to disclose any potential conflict of interest at each board meeting. They also require board members to recuse themselves from discussions—in some cases, they must actually leave the boardroom—that can potentially yield an outcome in which a member has a personal interest. Further, most board members are required to sign confidentiality statements that signify their agreement to keep information shared in the boardroom confidential during, and after, their terms of service.

> As healthcare board members you are being painted with the same brush— and viewed just as suspiciously— as those board members and healthcare organizations that have crossed ethical or legal lines.

Twenty years ago, such safeguards went a long way toward doing the job. Today, we are not so sure that is the case anymore. However, we are not suggesting that today's board member is any less ethical than his or her predecessors. In fact, we believe that the vast majority of board members are ethical individuals who have no intention of self-dealing or getting involved in any other unethical behavior. Rather, we contend that the issues that fall into the "gray zone"—where the ethical lines are much less clear—are increasing. Further, we believe that a few rotten apples are spoiling the bunch. In other words, as healthcare board members, you are being painted with the same brush — and viewed just as suspiciously — as those board members and healthcare organizations that have crossed ethical or legal lines.

An excellent summation of today's spotlight on ethics and the burden it places on board members is an article by policy analyst Emily Friedman in the September/October 1999 issue of *Health Forum Journal*. In the article, "Where Was the Board?," Friedman called attention to the much-publicized ethical and legal debacles in U.S. hospitals in the past few years. Among the charges that have unfortunately become common fodder for headlines are:

- Medicare and fraud abuse investigations that resulted in multimillion dollar penalties and subsequent resignations and, in some cases, imprisonment of CEOs, CFOs, and other senior executives;
- other improper billing and kickbacks; and
- theft and embezzlement among senior hospital executives.

As the title of the article asks, "Where Was the Board" when such unethical activities were afoot? Friedman's contention is that in such cases, we are observing either the "innocent" board or the board that "dirties its hand." According to Friedman, the "innocent board is composed of know-nothings who are willingly kept in the dark by CEOs and other executives who keep assuring them that everything is peachy-keen and they shouldn't worry their pretty little heads about it." Further, the "innocent board [will] accept the choice of the auditor and the audit report … approve all the recommendations they are handed without asking too much about them … trust the financial reports they are given …. enjoy the golf outings …. and they don't make trouble."

In contrast, the board "that dirties its hand" has trustees "who are themselves involved in either unethical or illegal activity."

Friedman wrote: "Trustees who knowingly approve the hiring of weak auditors, who wink at billing and other fraud, and who keep silent in return for a portion of the spoils are not only breaking the law and their own commitments as trustees; they are making it harder for every single health care trustee in this country."

We couldn't agree more. The glare of the ethical spotlight on you as a board member has never been greater and the tolerance for improper behavior has never been lesser. The government's full bench press to combat Medicare and Medicaid fraud is a case in point. Although the government has somewhat conceded that its compliance rules for Medicare and Medicaid participants are perhaps overly complex and ambiguous, it has every intention of uncovering and prosecuting in cases of wrongdoing.

Let's even engage in wishful thinking for a moment. Let's say that the government continues to investigate cases of alleged wrongdoing with zeal, but it prosecutes only cases that are considered flagrant abuses of the law. How much pride can you take as a board member of an organization that was even the subject of an investigation? Friedman put it this way: "I would like to think that not being indicted or convicted is not the highest ethical standard to which a health care organization should aspire."

Our research suggested that boards that "dirty their hands" are thankfully in the small minority. We are concerned, however, that "innocent boards" continue to be quite prevalent. In our opinion, innocent boards are the byproduct of (1) an organization that has never had "any trouble," so it assumes that its board members have served it well over time and will continue to do so; and/or (2) an organization that believes its legal and regulatory realities are too complex for its board members to grasp, so its management assumes the responsibility of ensuring that the organization does not go astray.

Both assumptions are dangerous and potentially disastrous. Calm waters of past days are absolutely no assurance of smooth sailing in the future. And if you assume the legal and regulatory realities of the day that could catapult your organization into peril are "too complex" for your board to grasp, you are either not doing enough to educate your board or you have board members who shouldn't be board members.

If you assume the legal and regula-
tory realities of the day that could catapult your organization into peril are "too complex" for your board to grasp, you are either not doing enough to educate your board or you have board members who shouldn't be board members.

Camcare's Phillip Goodwin offered this perspective: "Board members enjoy the visibility and prestige of being associated with a big corporate enterprise that is doing good work in a community. Then, one day they wake up and find out they made a bad deal with doctors, and they end up in jail with a $50,000 criminal penalty. If you don't tell your board members what they could be potentially held liable for—even face criminal prosecution for—then you are doing them a huge disservice."

The bottom line is that even if you are not directly involved in what is ultimately deemed an unethical or illegal act, even if you did not personally profit from the act, and even if you did not understand or were unaware of what was transpiring, you may not be immune from public criticism or, worse yet, legal action.

To CEOs: Do not be complacent and assume that you will protect your board members simply by having them sign conflict-of-interest and confidentiality statements.

Given the current state of healthcare affairs, we have advice for both CEOs and boards. To CEOs: Do not be complacent and assume that you will protect your board members simply by having them sign conflict-of-interest and confidentiality statements. Complying with those statements protects them in only a very small way. Instead, commit to continuously educating your board on potential ethical and legal quagmires. Make sure board members have a basic understanding of Medicare and Medicaid compliance, HIPAA regulations, and statutes governing referrals and other relationships between healthcare providers. Periodically share with the board press clippings that illustrate the consequences of not remaining vigilant about the laws governing the organization's operation.

To board members: Don't be afraid to ask questions.

To board members: Don't be afraid to ask questions. We are not encouraging you to become micro-managers; but at the same time, you must guard against "rubber stamping" everything. Yes, you may be perceived as the "squeaky wheel" because of your questions; and yes, at times, you may slow the decision-making process, but the consequences of complacency are potentially far more serious.

We recognize that this chapter is not terribly uplifting and it may be downright scary. Unfortunately, times are such that we must devote an entire chapter to ethical issues. But in fairness to those of you who willingly sign on for board service with a commitment of doing good for the organization and the community it serves, we believe our message is one you need to hear and take to heart. After all, good intentions are no longer enough.

Your questions may slow the decision-making process, but the consequences of complacency are potentially far more serious.

9

Board Education

No one disputes the value of board education. CEOs understand its importance and so do boards. At the risk of ruffling a few feathers, we would like to go on record and say that despite its recognized value, board education is highly unimaginative, too infrequent, and largely ineffective.

Mediocrity in board education is a result of it becoming largely routinized. Year after year, the agenda for new board member orientation remains largely unchanged, with the staff presenting virtually the same reference materials and virtually the same "overviews." And, as day-to-day pressure increases, we have observed a corresponding decrease in the amount of time devoted to both orientations and periodic board-education programs.

In some ways this is ironic. When you consider that the board is the policymaking body charged with keeping the organization on course and setting future directions, ensuring that board members were prepared for such a daunting task would seem to be of the utmost importance. Yet, board education is one activity that constantly gets more lip service than meaningful attention.

Our view is apparently shared by CEOs nationwide. The survey by AHA and Ernst & Young LLP reported that 42 percent of CEOs thought that improvement of board education in the next few years was "very important" and "essential." Since the survey

> Despite its recognized value, board education is highly unimaginative, too infrequent, and largely ineffective.

85

published nearly three years ago, we hope that improvements are afoot, although more are clearly warranted.

In our view, board education has three important components—(1) orientation for new board members; (2) ongoing education that takes place at regular board meetings; and (3) board retreats, which provide an opportunity for board members to interact formally and collegially and address the big-picture issues that may not get addressed during the course of regular board meetings.

ORIENTATION FOR NEW BOARD MEMBERS

If you have managed to fit your orientation for new board members into a single day, then you either have a remarkably simple organizational structure or you have truncated the program to the point that it qualifies as an orientation only in name. Even the most brilliant board members or those who are known to be "quick studies" will find it difficult to digest all they need to know so quickly. Trying to cover the waterfront in a day's time will undoubtedly result in information overload and not achieve your intended purpose.

Board education should be multifaceted and be held over a period of several days, for three to four hours at a time. During the course of our interviews, we spoke with Frank V. Sacco, FACHE, CEO of Memorial Healthcare System. Sacco provides his new board members with a 13-hour orientation held over the course of three days. The program involves both information sharing and tours of Memorial Healthcare's hospitals.

Although other key staff members participate in the program, Sacco personally plays a key role in the orientation. We cannot overemphasize the importance of the CEO's involvement. His or her involvement sends an important message—the orientation is not a perfunctory exercise but well-worth the board members' and the CEO's time. In addition, the CEO's presence provides a comfortable forum in which new board members can ask the

When you consider that the board is the policymaking body charged with keeping the organization on course and setting future directions, ensuring that board members were prepared for such a daunting task would seem to be of the utmost importance. Yet, board education is one activity that constantly gets more lip service than meaningful attention.

CEO questions that they might be hesitant to ask at their first board meeting.

The inclusion of site visits is another notable aspect of Sacco's orientation program. Touring the entities that they govern helps emphasize to the board members the importance of their responsibility and humanize the organizations whose futures they will ultimately influence.

Whether you are ready to embrace Sacco's all-inclusive approach to orientation or have a slightly less-ambitious game plan, you will want to include, at a minimum, the following reference materials in your orientation:

- a healthcare industry overview, with emphasis on service area trends (e.g., glossary of commonly used "business healthcare terms");
- organizational overview (e.g., strategic plan, recent annual report, organizational charts, bylaws, and board "job description");
- financial overview (e.g., most recent budget or report of key financial indicators);
- medical staff and quality assurance overview (i.e., credentialing documents);
- legal overview (i.e., summary of key federal regulations and law; for example, compliance); and
- issue overview (e.g., documents that address key issues currently being considered by the board).

See Appendix F for a sample new board member orientation agenda from John C. Lincoln Health Network.

ONGOING BOARD EDUCATION

Just as healthcare executives stay ahead of the curve by reading trade journals and other business publications and by periodically

> If you have managed to fit your orientation for new board members in a single day, then you either have a remarkably simple organizational structure or you have truncated the program to the point that it qualifies as an orientation only in name.

> Touring the entities that they govern helps emphasize to the board members the importance of their responsibility and humanize the organizations whose futures they will ultimately influence.

attending professional-development programs, so too must board members have the benefit of ongoing education.

A number of the CEOs we interviewed allot time for board education at every board meeting. For example, if the topic of the meeting is managed care update, the CEO can provide an update on managed care penetration in the service area, the organization's managed care market share, and emerging models of managed care being offered currently. Similarly, if the topic is the Balanced Budget Act, the CEO or CFO can provide an update on the BBA's effects on the organization, which can then be factored into future planning and policy decisions. The range of topics is endless when you consider how quickly the health-care landscape changes.

Perhaps one of the easiest ways to keep the board up-to-speed is to include pertinent articles from both general and trade publications in each agenda packet. Whether the publication is *Harvard Business Review* or *Modern Healthcare*, something of interest and value is likely present in virtually every issue and merits inclusion in the agenda packet. In addition, many board members find a subscription to *Trustee* to be very helpful.

BOARD RETREATS

One of the first perquisites that a new board member learns about are the board retreats. Why? It's simple. Board retreats are considered the "reward" for board service. They are often held in tropical paradises, include lavish meals, and are a combination of work and play.

Don't get us wrong; we have no problem with board members being rewarded for their hard work, and we believe that both formal and informal interactions between management and board members are valuable. However, the key to a productive board retreat is if the board members return to their organizations with a renewed commitment to their board work and new insights that will make them more effective board members.

Most CEOs and board chairs we interviewed highly recommended the programs offered by both The Governance Institute, based in La Jolla, California, and Estes Park Institute, based in Englewood, Colorado. In addition, a number of our interviewees have also attended and found valuable the Partnership Institute—a program for teams of board chairs, CEOs, and medical staff leaders offered by the American College of Healthcare Executives. The upside of these programs is that their presenters are distinguished speakers with expertise in governance; they cover key governance issues of interest to board members, regardless of the types of organizations they govern; their participants receive a wealth of useful reference materials; and, frankly, they are typically held in wonderful locations.

The downside of these programs is that they are relatively expensive (ranging from roughly $900 to $1,300 per person, excluding travel and lodging); they run upwards of three days; and they are not designed to address in any great detail a specific organization's governance issues. As a result, these programs may be a difficult proposition for financially strapped institutions or those where board members cannot afford to be away from their jobs for more than a day at a time.

In a perfect world, in which we acknowledge few healthcare organizations can claim to live, we believe that holding two board retreats annually is valuable (although we recognize that this ideal is hard to achieve). These retreats can include attendance at a general governance program such as those described above and attendance at a one- or two-day off-site program to address specific organizational governance issues. One-day off-site retreats are particularly ideal to kick off the organization's strategic planning process. Strategic planning, which is discussed in Chapter 13, is an integral part of the board's responsibility to

> The key to a productive board retreat is if the board members return to their organizations with a renewed commitment to their board work and new insights that will make them more effective board members.

the organization and a retreat affords the board an opportunity to step back without significant time restraints to look to the future. CEOs have differing opinions about the value of hiring independent consultants or facilitators to lead such retreats. That is really a personal decision. Certainly, consultants can bring objectivity to the discussion and keep the board focused and moving forward. Further, consultants are freer to deliver "tough news" to the board than can the CEO. On the other hand, consultants lack the organizational knowledge that some CEOs and boards deem important to frame the discussion, and, of course, they cost money. Whether or not you are in favor of hiring a consultant, committing to at least one, if not two, retreats a year is key to practical governance. We know of no CEO or board chair who has ever found a retreat to be a waste of time.

One-day off-site retreats are particularly ideal to kick off the organization's strategic planning process.

10
CEO Performance Appraisal

PROBABLY ONE OF the least enjoyed and least understood tasks of the board are the annual evaluations of the CEO. In too many instances, this process is entered into with much trepidation and little preparation. Each party to the process may feel that it is unfair and that the results are predictable. Sometimes when the board must convey unpleasant news regarding the performance of its CEO, the message can become hurtful and not be conveyed directly or appropriately. Several years ago, we conducted a study of CEO performance appraisal and found that one in ten CEOs never had a performance appraisal even though it is a JCAHO requirement and a prime indicator of good governance. Based on our findings, some of the factors that hinder the board from facilitating a good performance appraisal are:

- fear of confrontation;
- lack of clarity or agreement over the organization's vision, goals, or priorities;
- failure to explicitly define the totality of the CEO's responsibilities and authority;
- uncertainty regarding the appropriate criteria to be used in the assessment;

- necessity of investing a significant amount of time and energy in evaluating and providing feedback on the CEO's goal achievement and overall performance;

Affirm that the objective of the performance appraisal process is to support or change behavior.

- uncertainty regarding the board's responsibility in the CEO evaluation;
- concern that the special nature of the board CEO relationship will be disturbed;
- perception that tolerating an existing CEO is easier than chancing a disruption that change would cause; and
- lack of enough direct contact with the CEO to evaluate him or her on leadership behaviors and other "soft results."

The following are some suggestions we gleaned from our interviews and our experience with CEO performance appraisals. We think these suggestions will make the process fairer and more beneficial for all parties involved.

Affirm that the objective of the performance appraisal process is to support or change behavior. Boards commit the mistake of not defining the objective of the appraisal or mixing the objectives such that its end results are muddled. For example, a board might decide that the objective of the performance appraisal is to determine the CEO's salary for the next year. We believe that this objective is unfair and not comprehensive because performance is only one aspect of salary determination. (See Exhibit 10.1 for a comprehensive list of salary determinants.)

A board that practices practical governance might divorce the performance appraisal from compensation altogether if it really seeks to change CEO behavior. In this type of appraisal, a CEO might get a favorable review and no pay increase or vice versa. Another example is a board that has determined that the objective of the performance appraisal is to justify the firing of the CEO. Clearly, the firing of the CEO should never be a surprise.

Exhibit 10.1: Determinants of Compensation

- Overall performance of the organization
- Competitive salary evaluation vis à vis similar organizations
- Equity within the organization
- Inflation
- Length of time in position
- Risk or volatility of position
- Political or community considerations

"A leader is evidenced by the presence of willing followers."

—Peter Drucker

The CEO should have plenty of explicit warnings about the imminent firing, but oftentimes this is not the case.

Determine who gives input to the evaluation. Ideally you should seek input from a number of different sources. The CEO should certainly have input on his or her own evaluation by rating himself or herself against the same criteria used by the board. In addition, input can be sought from the medical staff leadership and other board members. Some organizations have implemented performance appraisal programs that also seek input from subordinates and from others. The 360-degree feedback, also known as a multirater system, is one of the most well-known performance appraisal instruments. We endorse a multirater system because it is inherently fair and appropriate in evaluating CEO performance. (See Appendix G for a sample multirater performance appraisal system.) A multirater system is especially effective in helping the board deal with that important, but elusive, concept of leadership. Often, the board evaluates leadership through its experience and perception of the CEO's ability to lead the board and its activities. In reality, however, leadership affects the entire organization, not just the board. To quote management guru Peter Drucker, "a leader is evidenced by the presence of willing followers." What better way to evaluate leadership ability than to ask the "followers" to rate the CEO?

The CEO should have plenty of explicit warnings about the imminent firing.

Regular feedback from the board chair or the board's executive committee allows the CEO to adjust behaviors or tactics before an issue becomes a major irritation for the board or the medical staff.

Remember that performance appraisal is an ongoing, and not just an annual, process. Issues should be addressed as they come up and not held until the annual performance appraisal. Regular feedback from the board chair or the board's executive committee allows the CEO to adjust behaviors or tactics before an issue becomes a major irritation for the board or the medical staff. This feedback should occur quarterly at least and often can be delivered informally over breakfast or lunch. More frequent feedback may be needed when a situation is especially fluid, which just about describes most aspects of healthcare today.

THE APPRAISAL PROCESS

Often, the board doesn't organize itself for the performance appraisal process until the date of the "sit-down" with the CEO. In actuality, the process should have begun a year earlier. The board must pose the following questions to initiate the process at the beginning of the CEO's tenure or anniversary year:

- What is going to be evaluated?
- Who is going to have input on the evaluation?
- What are the exact steps in the evaluation process?
- What methodology is going to be used? What evaluation instrument will be selected?
- Who is responsible for seeing that the evaluation process is kept on track?
- What is the objective of the evaluation process?
- How are the results of the process going to be communicated?

A meeting should be scheduled with the CEO to solicit input on the process and to discuss the above questions. That meeting should produce a timetable and agreement on the process and the factors to be evaluated.

When the question "Is the CEO doing his job?" arises at the beginning of a performance appraisal, the first reference that the board must consult is the CEO's job description. Ask the CEO to prepare or update his or her job description at the beginning of the year and have the description reviewed and approved by the executive committee. (See Appendix H for a sample CEO job description.)

Although boards often elect to evaluate the CEO on quantitative criteria alone, we believe that qualitative criteria are also important for a meaningful assessment; these criteria can be evaluated through use of a multirater system. Following are some of the quantitative measures that are most frequently used by boards:

- financial performance against budget, in accounts receivable, current ratio, debt/equity ratio, etc.;
- operating indicators such as length of stay, average daily census, admissions, outpatient visits, etc.;
- physician satisfaction as evidenced by survey scores; and
- employee satisfaction as evidenced by survey scores.

In recent years, the American College of Healthcare Executives (ACHE) has put renewed emphasis on holding the CEO accountable for community health status. ACHE affirmed its stance in its 1993 monograph *Evaluating the Performance of the Hospital CEO in a Total Quality Management Environment*. Today, more CEOs are seeing community health status and community needs appear on their performance appraisal objectives. One of our interviewees, Peter Bastone, president and CEO of Mission Hospital, said: "I am evaluated annually by the board's executive committee, and it is extremely helpful because the committee has a big-picture view of my effectiveness. They aren't only concerned with whether I am running the organization well in terms of operations, but also in the role I play in making sure my organization is meeting community needs." In the monograph, ACHE also noted two other major categories for evaluation: (1) institutional success and (2) professional role fulfillment. Under "Institutional Success," the criteria were:

1. planning;
2. human resources management;
3. quality healthcare services;
4. fiscal management;
5. compliance with regulation;
6. advocacy;
7. promotion of the hospital; and
8. leadership ability.

Under "Professional Role Fulfillment," the criteria included continuing education and mentoring.

In addition, the board may also quantitatively evaluate the CEO on how well he or she accomplished tasks set out by the board at the beginning of the evaluation period. These tasks are typically evaluated by the percentage of completion; the rate of completion then becomes the basis for some type of a bonus. A note of caution to the board: Letting the achievement of a bonus indicate that a CEO is doing a good job is tempting. In our view, the achievement of a bonus is only one indicator of good performance; we can point to many CEOs who have been fired after receiving such bonuses.

One of our favorite factors to evaluate is how well the CEO "lives" the mission of the organization. Sometimes CEOs get caught up in the heat of the battle and fail to note that they, along with the board, have lost sight of the mission in their quest to successfully conduct everyday business. Evaluating the CEO against the mission of the organization at least annually gives the leadership an opportunity to contemplate the mission and to assess if it is being followed. During this time, updating the mission and determining its relevancy to the current situation and mindset of the organization is a good idea. A good multirater system makes this kind of evaluation a breeze. The Catholic Health Association produced a multirater system for evaluating management in Catholic healthcare systems in accordance with Catholic values. This system has been incorporated in many CEO performance appraisals.

Whether you decide to use a multirater system or other types of assessment tools, the information you glean from the process must be communicated to the CEO. This is typically done at a formal meeting between the board's executive committee and the CEO. In the meeting, the information is discussed and the CEO's feedback and comments are noted.

Most CEOs would like to have the opportunity to give written, as well as oral, feedback to the committee. A multirater system accomplishes this easily, but other systems can also work. After the discussion, the onus is on the CEO to develop an action plan based on the results of the discussion and to have the executive committee approve the plan. This plan would then become a part of the next year's evaluation process. The committee would then communicate to the board the results of the process. Communication between these parties during this time is especially sensitive.

Sending a letter to the CEO confirming the discussions and recapturing the comments is a common practice. This letter becomes a part of the CEO's personnel file. Care must be taken in drafting this letter to ensure that the essence of the conversations is captured. Too often, we have reviewed letters to CEOs that contained only minimal hints of the board's serious dissatisfaction with the CEO.

The board's responsibility is to communicate effectively, frequently, and candidly with the CEO. The CEO's responsibility, in turn, is to take action and make changes. Ensuring that the performance appraisal process is fair and covers all the bases is the responsibility of both the board and the CEO.

> **The board's responsibility is to communicate effectively, frequently, and candidly with the CEO. The CEO's responsibility, in turn, is to take action and make changes. Ensuring that the performance appraisal process is fair and covers all the bases is the responsibility of both the board and the CEO.**

Board Evaluations

DO BOARDS NEED to periodically evaluate how they are doing? Absolutely. Virtually all CEOs we interviewed said their boards conduct self-assessments annually. Almost all of them said the evaluations were quite helpful. The board chairs we interviewed agreed.

That said, we are not convinced that board self-assessments, the most commonly used means of evaluation, are all that enlightening or helpful. But before we explain our reservations about the self-assessment process, we want to first explain what these assessments tend to look like and how they are used.

As James E. Orlikoff and Mary K. Totten (1998) point out in their book, *Trustee Handbook for Health Care Governance*, self-assessments typically provide board members with an opportunity to address the following questions:

- What are we doing well?
- What could we be doing better?
- What are our objectives?
- How well did we achieve our objectives?
- Why didn't we achieve our objectives?

Most self-assessment instruments are questionnaires or surveys that are closed-ended with multiple-choice answer options and additional space for comments. Questions typically address board concerns such as how well board meetings are attended, whether the level of participation is good, if major organizational issues are addressed, and whether the board is effective in furthering the organization's mission. Our review of many of these instruments revealed to us that the scenarios or questions posed are worded in a way that the board can, in good conscience, answer that it is doing a good job all-in-all. Unless a board's performance is absolutely abysmal, chances are it can give itself pretty good ratings in each of the areas addressed.

Unfortunately, many self-assessments fail to ask the tough questions—questions that force the board to examine its "real" accomplishments in establishing a future direction for the organization and in fulfilling its overall fiduciary responsibility. The most obvious reasons, at least to us, some of these tough questions aren't asked are that (1) insufficient time is allotted for completion of the assessments and (2) at the end of the year, the board is unlikely to have sufficient recall of many of the key outcomes of meetings held as much as 12 months earlier.

We recognize that by the time the board members reach the last item on the board agenda, they often begin packing up their materials and readying themselves to get out the door. That is understandable after having just spent a good three or four hours deliberating hard on issues that are often controversial and not always clear cut. But let's face it, the conclusion of the meeting is the time when the high and low points of the meeting are freshest in the board's minds. After the meeting is when board members are best able to evaluate whether the meeting was a good use of their time, whether it yielded useful outcomes, whether everyone was prepared, whether the CEO did his or her job well, and whether the board chair effectively moved the meeting along.

So what are we suggesting? Our suggestion, one that frankly was championed by some of our CEO interviewees and dismissed

> Unfortunately, many self-assessments fail to ask the tough questions— questions that force the board to examine its "real" accomplishments in establishing a future direction for the organization and in fulfilling its overall fiduciary responsibility.

by others, is this: Although boards have traditionally been discouraged from conducting a self-assessment after each meeting, we suggest that at the end of each meeting, each board member should be asked to fill out a brief—no more than a single page—self-assessment form. The form can be either mailed or faxed before, or brought into, the next meeting. Completing the assessments must be an implicit expectation of board service, not an "if-you-wouldn't-mind" request. To encourage honest, candid responses, we recommend that the assessments be anonymous and be a combination of open-ended and closed-ended questions. (See Appendix I for a sample board and board meeting self-assessment instrument.)

If you are skeptical about the feasibility or desirability of giving the board a self-assessment at the end of every meeting, here are some additional benefits to consider:

1. *Frequent assessments allow for mid-course corrections.* An assessment conducted at year's end may highlight impediments to governance effectiveness. This year-end assessment might reveal that a whole year has gone by without the board having taken action to address these deficiencies. In contrast, if assessments from two or three meetings identify similar concerns, you have an opportunity to "strike while the iron is hot" and not repeat mistakes for the remainder of the year.

2. *The CEO and board chair have a "heads up" when they are not fulfilling the board's expectations of them.* We know of few CEOs who would prefer to find out their shortcomings during their annual performance reviews. Similarly, through our interviews we heard a lot about various board chair's "style," with comments ranging from "arrogant" to "ineffective" to "wonderful." We believe that board chairs would prefer to have their legacies fall in the "wonderful"

Although boards have traditionally been discouraged from conducting a self-assessment after each meeting, we suggest that at the end of each meeting, each board member should be asked to fill out a brief form.

If assessments from two or three meetings identify similar concerns, you have an opportunity to "strike while the iron is hot" and not repeat mistakes in the course of the year.

category, but if they don't receive feedback until after completing their first year of service, they have less opportunity to rise to the occasion.

3. *Meeting-by-meeting evaluations provide detailed feedback rather than vague recollections about board accomplishments.* Why is this evaluation important? First, it offers you a historical record and some longitudinal data about board effectiveness. Second, if you use the assessments to develop a summary of board accomplishments, they can be extremely useful to new board members because they reveal the "lay of the land" of board work.

If you still aren't convinced that meeting-by-meeting assessments are the way to go, so be it. If that is the case, certainly continue your annual assessments. They are not without some value. We urge you, though, to revisit your current assessment and review past results. After your review, if you conclude that the results are "exactly as you expected" and that you "didn't really learn anything," then now is probably the time to redesign the assessment. After all, asking questions makes no sense if you already have the answers.

BEYOND THE SELF-ASSESSMENT

Certainly, even the best self-assessment instrument provides only limited insight into governance effectiveness. This tends to be the case because much of what contributes to board dysfunction is what everyone knows to be true but few comfortably acknowledge. Or, even if these deficiencies are highlighted through the assessment process, they are not typically accusatory in nature and don't zero in on the board member, or members, who isn't performing well. From our interviews and personal observation, we gleaned three major causes of board dysfunction:

1. insufficient preparation by the CEO or management staff in advance of the meeting;
2. an effective or overbearing board chair; and
3. certain board members who consistently are not prepared for meetings or are repeated obstructionists.

The easiest cause to address is the one related to insufficient preparation. Luckily, this is a common but not prevalent problem. How long should you let insufficient preparation compromise the board meeting's value? Easy—once and only once. Most likely, the CEO will also recognize that more meeting preparation is in order and make sure that lack of preparation does not happen again. If the CEO didn't pick up on the problem, then the board probably has a bigger problem than inadequate meeting preparation, and the board chair needs to intervene. We are not suggesting a public bloodletting, but rather a private discussion about the need for better preparation in the future. To this end, the board chair should be as specific as possible about expectations (e.g., how far in advance board members should receive their agenda packets, what level of detail should be included, etc.)

The issue of having an ineffective or overbearing board chair is somewhat more difficult to address. Most of the CEOs we interviewed have had a board chair who fit one (ineffective) or the other (overbearing) description at least once in his or her career. What usually happens in these cases is one of three things: nothing, the CEO intervenes, or board members intervene. Obviously, nothing is not the preferred option, and CEO intervention, if not handled properly, can prove to be a career-limiting move. Yet, if you don't have board members who are willing to speak up, then unfortunately it becomes the CEO's responsibility.

One CEO we spoke with shared this description of his previous board chair: "To put it nicely, he was a bit on the wishy-washy side. Board members often wandered into discussions of operational issues. Instead of standing up and saying 'Wait a minute, this is a management issue, not one for us to discuss,' he would just let it go and let the board beat on it until it died. Then, after the board meeting, he would say to me, 'I guess I didn't stand up and defend you, did I?' I'd be honest and say, 'No, you left me out on a limb again.' He was our board chairman for two years. It wasn't until the end of his term that he understood how to be an effective board chairman."

> **In the perfect world, board members would help the board chair to become a good chair.**

Another CEO told us of a previous board chair who was in the position for six years. The CEO said: "I think it is fair to say that he ran roughshod over the board, and, as a result, the board did not function very effectively. The current board chairman, probably in part in reaction to his predecessor, has opened the process up."

> **"When people start talking about the little stuff, then you know they don't have enough to do and are going to be a real pain."**

In the perfect world, which we referred to before and acknowledged does not exist, board members would help the board chair to become a good chair. They may not win the chair's adoration by pointing out that his or her leadership approach could use some rethinking, but ultimately the result will be a more effective board.

The most common type of board dysfunction, which is not insurmountable, is when the board has members who are under-achievers or obstructionists. One solution is to wait out their term and then send them packing. Clearly, this is not the ideal solution. Unfortunately, only a handful of CEOs we talked with said that their board members are uniformly strong—relatively equal contributors to the process. One board chair lamented: "I would say about half the board gets it—really understands or even cares what's going on. The other half appears to have too much time on their hands. When people start talking about the little stuff, then you know they don't have enough to do and are going to be a real pain." We heard similar comments from many other CEOs and board chairs. We also heard plenty about obstructionist board members who tend to see things as "black" when the rest of the board see things as "white." They become predictable to the point where their input is almost routinely discounted. When they get the floor, other board members pull out their hand-held computers to check their e-mails or excuse themselves from the room to make an "important phone call."

Obstructionist board members are probably a fact of life. Yet, how one rotten apple can spoil the bunch is amazing. For that reason, we are strong proponents of "self-correcting boards," where each board member feels a personal responsibility for making the meeting effective, including taking the initiative to speak up when another board member is preventing that from happening.

Again, we are not advocates of public humiliation. At the same time, however, depending on the level of interference with board operations that an individual is causing, confrontation may not be something that can wait until the conclusion of the meeting. (This is most true in the case of obstructionists. Noncontributing board members are probably better dealt with privately.) Exhibit 11.1 provides some strategies you might employ if you were faced with an obstructionist.

We are strong proponents of "self-correcting boards," where each board member feels a personal responsibility for making the meeting effective, including taking the initiative to speak up when another board member is preventing that from happening.

Exhibit 11.1: How to Deal with an Obstructionist Board Member

1. Be direct and communicate that the comments being made are not germane to the issue or are on a topic that is not under the board's purview.
2. Ask questions that will force the individual to defend his or her position, rather than simply make unsupported statements.
3. Suggest that the individual listen to others' opinions before reaching a conclusion.
4. Urge the board chair to limit the amount of time each board member can spend on the topic at hand to ensure the discussion moves along and a decision can be reached.

Although none of the strategies in Exhibit 11.1 is guaranteed to work each time, you will find that if you are consistent and out front in dealing with obstructionist board members, they will eventually get the point. No one wants to be labeled an "obstructionist," even if they are one. By sending clear, repeated signals to such individuals, we are willing to bet you will see the board member's behavior improve for the better.

12

CEO Selection, Contracts, and Succession Planning

OF ALL THE board activities, perhaps the most important is the selection of the CEO. No other board activity has such a dramatic impact on the lives and careers of the members of the healthcare organization and on the healthcare of the community. Therefore, like marriage, it is not an activity to be entered into lightly.

The process of selecting a CEO is every bit as important as its outcome. In fact, the selection of the CEO is a process that needs to involve many constituency groups; otherwise, the outcome may be either in doubt or tainted. In order to achieve a good outcome, a board must carefully manage the selection process so that its end result garners the support of most, if not all, of the organization's constituencies. The selection process gives validity to the results. Therefore, pay attention to your CEO selection process and you will increase your chances of selecting the *right* CEO.

THE SELECTION PROCESS

Selecting and Charging the Search Committee

A board would typically begin the process by selecting a search committee made up of not more than five people. A typical committee would consist of:

- a board chair;
- a medical staff president;
- a medical staff president-elect; and
- two other members, usually from the board.

Just because a constituency group does not have a member on the committee doesn't mean that the group cannot have input.

The chair of the committee is often the current board chair, but doesn't have to be. If the current board chair is not chair of the committee, then the board chair typically sits as a member of the committee. The role of the committee chair is to ensure that the committee does its work on a timely basis, to coordinate with any search firm involved, to make committee assignments, and to communicate the actions of the committee to the board and medical staff. The search committee chair is typically the only public voice of the committee, so the other members of the committee should respect this designation and not "talk out of school."

The committee's charge is to make a recommendation to the board on who should be the next CEO of the hospital. In addition, the committee may be charged with recommending a compensation package and negotiating a contract with the new CEO. Sometimes the committee is charged with recommending more than one candidate to the board, which in turn makes the decision from that pool of candidates. We believe that if the process is handled correctly, the committee should be charged with bringing forth only one candidate—the unanimous choice of the committee.

The board should avoid the tendency to add to the committee a representative from each of the various constituency groups in the organization. This would cause the committee to be too large and unwieldy and automatically make scheduling meetings harder. This scheduling conflict almost ensures that all of the committee members may not meet all of the candidates. Just because a constituency group does not have a member on the committee doesn't mean that the group cannot have input. As an example, the hospital auxiliary is important to the healthcare organization's mission and delivery system. Representatives of this group can give input on new CEO specification at the start of the search and during the latter parts of the process, can interview the finalists, and can give general input without being on the committee.

The CEO search process will take at least 120 days and up to a year. Representatives selected should be able to commit to an extended process, at least six meetings of the committee, and perhaps some individual assignments during the course of the process.

THE SEARCH PROCESS

Developing the Specifications

During the first phase of the search, the committee must develop a job description to give to the candidates and also must reach consensus on the background and behavioral characteristics of the ideal candidate. As an example, a common decision point would be whether the committee would seek only sitting CEOs or whether it will interview COOs at similar-sized and larger organizations. Try to keep your specifications reasonable and limit behavioral characteristics to about 12.

Recruiting the Candidates

Most committees either employ a search firm to recruit for them or do the recruitment themselves by running ads or soliciting referrals from individuals they trust. Most board chairs we interviewed said that their organizations typically use the services of retained executive search firms. Search firms bring a formalized process of conducting the search, the manpower needed to do the legwork on the search, objectivity, and a network of potentially viable candidates. They also have a process to help keep the search from going awry.

Key Elements of the Search Firm RFP

• A job description or "performance expectations" of the CEO
• Background on the organization, including documents such as the vision and mission statements and strategic plan
• Information regarding the search parameters such as time lines
• Committee's expectations of the search firm

Key to your satisfaction with the search firm is your ability to clearly articulate your expectations.

If you decided to employ an executive search firm, your first charge is to find the firm that best meets your organization's needs. A common and a good way to start this is by sending a request for proposals (RFP) to search firms being considered for the assignment.

Among other things, the committee will want to pay attention to how thoroughly the firm responded to the RFP; the firm's past client list and if the clients include organizations of similar complexity to the committee's organization; and who in the firm will be conducting the search. In addition, the committee will want to examine whether the RFP response appears to be a "cookie-cutter" response or if it reflects the firm's effort to understand the organization and its specific needs.

Following the review of the RFP responses, the slate of potential firms to be engaged should be narrowed to two or three. Then, each of these firms should be invited to make presentations of about an hour to the committee. Make sure that those presenting are those who would actually be involved in the search. This way, you can assess the consultants' expertise and get a sense of whether you will be comfortable working closely with them for the duration of the search.

Key to your satisfaction with the search firm is your ability to clearly articulate your expectations. The leading cause of dissatisfaction with search firms isn't that they fail to produce viable candidates, but rather that their approach is not what the committee envisioned. By being direct and specific about your expectations, you will spare all involved a lot of unnecessary frustration. Alfred Zeien, former chair and CEO of Gillette, put it this way in a 1999 discussion in the *Harvard Business Review:* "I've found that the search firm is only as good as the specification it receives from the board."

When evaluating search firms remember that it is unethical for a search firm to recruit from its client organizations. If a search firm has too many clients, it will not have anywhere to go to solicit candidates without violating its "off-limits" policy. In an executive search, too little or too much experience are negatives.

If you decided to recruit on your own, make sure that the candidates are treated professionally and that someone is in charge of talking with the candidates, sending them the job description and specifications, soliciting more information, and bringing the collected information to the committee. These duties should either be assigned to the committee member who has the most time or should be doled out to committee members equally. Committees that recruit on their own typically interview many more candidates than they would interview when using a search firm.

Interviewing the Candidates

The process of interviewing candidates is typically divided into two parts—the first and second interviews. The first interview is usually done by the committee members alone. We recommend that for the first interview, the committee members individually interview the candidates, not as a whole committee. A one-on-one interview is the best possible way to get to know a candidate. After the first interview, the committee would get together to compare notes and select which candidates to bring back for second interviews. Usually at this time, the candidate field is cut in half.

On the second interview, the entire committee would interview as one body for a couple of hours, firing questions at the

When evaluating search firms remember that it is unethical for a search firm to recruit from its client organizations.

candidate and answering any questions the candidate might have. The second interview becomes very important because after it is completed, the committee will have to come to a conclusion on whom to offer the position. Additionally, this is also the time to introduce the candidate to others in the organization whose input is valuable. The second interview should include meetings with the entire medical staff leadership (usually for breakfast), the executive staff (usually for lunch), and members of the board who are not on the committee. The meeting with board members is usually done informally, with refreshments, such that the board members can shake hands, engage in informal conversation, and be disengaged quickly.

The second interview normally would include the spouse, so the scheduling must be coordinated to allow the candidate time with the spouse to look at real estate and to allow the spouse time to socialize with spouses of the committee members. During this round, everyone involved in the process must remember that CEO selection is a two-way street: You are selecting the CEO and he or she is selecting you. Committee members should, at some point, remove their selection hats and put on their recruiting hats. Nothing is more frustrating for the committee than going through a recruiting process and being turned down when an offer is made. Most often, the turndowns come because the committee didn't sell the position or the community when the opportunity presented itself.

As a condition of practical governance, we recommend that the chair and another member of the committee meet with the candidate immediately after the formal committee interview is over to discuss salary and benefit parameters with the candidate. We believe that part of the selection process is determining how much a candidate is going to cost the organization, so it should be discussed during the process and not after the selection has been made. Some candidates offer such good values that they are preferable over marginally better candidates whose compensation levels might be achieved by the organization only through immense agony and with the possibility of negative publicity.

Checking References

No selection
process is
complete until
references have
been checked.

No selection process is complete until references have been checked. No matter how much you like the candidates or how much pressure your committee is under to complete its work, referencing is a necessary and important part of a search. To fail to check references is to hire in peril. References fall into four categories:

Letters of refer-
ence are usually
discounted
and are known
primarily for what
they don't say
instead of what
they do say.

1. supervisors;
2. peers;
3. subordinates; and
4. others (e.g., physicians, consultants, board members, lawyers, etc.).

Ideally, the committee should check references in all categories, but emphasis should be placed on the supervisory category. Often, the committee breaks down the referencing such that each committee member checks at least one reference on each candidate. Letters of reference are usually discounted and are known primarily for what they don't say instead of what they do say.

We think that checking references in phases is the best way to go. This means that the committee would check references at various stages of the process, and that the final offer would be made contingent upon a final reference check of the current employer. In the latter stages, the committee should call individuals who were not given as a reference by the candidate. This is a very tricky situation because the committee doesn't want to be responsible for causing the candidate to lose his or her current position. Nevertheless, the committee doesn't want to be blindsided if negative information is revealed by other sources. Other checks, beside for references, are also important in the final stages prior to an offer. Criminal and credit checks are extremely important for a CEO, and the committee chair should ensure that someone has verified the degrees, certifications, or affiliations with the appropriate schools and professional societies.

OFFER, NEGOTIATION, AND ACCEPTANCE

If the committee performs its work well, then usually the end is anticlimactic; that is, everyone is on board, the offer is made to the consensus candidate, and the acceptance comes quickly. Typically, the committee meets, discusses the candidates in depth, takes a vote, and decides to offer the position to one of the candidates. Occasionally, the committee is very divided about the candidates. If the committee can't decide, it should do one of two things: (1) invite the candidates back for third interviews or (2) start the whole process over. We hope the latter will not happen and a consensus will be reached for one candidate. After the vote is taken and a consensus has emerged, then someone on the committee usually makes a motion to recommend the candidate to the board, and the committee votes to make it a unanimous recommendation.

Negotiations typically start immediately upon board approval of the candidate and are usually headed by the committee chair and the board chair. If they are one and the same, then members of the committee participate. If the chair of the personnel and compensation committee happens to be on the search committee, then that individual participates.

As a starting point, the committee should review the CEO contract recommended by the American College of Healthcare Executives, which is discussed later in this chapter. We believe that the committee chair should have had preliminary discussions with the candidate regarding compensation and benefits during the interview process so that the negotiations that follow are really oriented toward putting everything into writing.

CONCLUDING EVENTS

Yogi Berra used to say "It ain't over 'til it's over." In an executive search, the recruiting process is not over until the candidate reports to work. Do not relax until your committee chair has a signed contract in his or her hands. In today's healthcare world, excellent CEOs are in high demand. Chances are that the CEO's current organization doesn't want to lose him or her. A counter offer may be in the cards and may catch the committee unaware. Remain in touch with your candidate, and make sure that all of the paperwork is moving along smoothly. Ask the candidate how the resignation went with his or her current board chair or supervisor. Have periodic contact with the spouse. Gauge the "climate." Is everything friendly and upbeat or is it guarded? Are there unexplained gaps between contacts? Don't issue a media release until you are absolutely sure that the CEO is coming. Even then, make sure that the CEO participates in the development of the media release and approves its wording.

> In an executive search, the recruiting process is not over until the candidate reports to work.

After all is said and done, CEO selection also involves a bit of good fortune. Memorial Health System's board chair, Terry Gerber, put it this way: "I was on the committee that selected Phil Newbold. We had three very good candidates whom we might have chosen and who could have probably done the job very well. When I look back, I think 'Thank goodness we hired Phil.' We had done our homework, but it was also a bit of luck that we got Phil, who has exceeded our high expectations."

CEO CONTRACTS

The value of CEO contracts cannot be overstated. It provides both the organization and the CEO with the assurances that they need in today's volatile healthcare marketplace. Customarily, the CEO of a healthcare organization will be presented with an employment contract. A contract is a necessary tool for keeping a CEO engaged in doing what is necessary to advance the organization and to minimize his or her tendency to do nothing for fear of losing the job.

The American College of Healthcare Executives has produced several publications on employment contracts for CEOs; the most recent of them are referenced in Appendix A. The publications are a far more comprehensive discussion than what we have highlighted in this chapter and would be good reading for those who have not yet given a contract to their CEO and are contemplating doing so.

Some people think that a CEO contract is only good for the CEO and that the organization gets no benefit for its efforts in putting the CEO under a contract. This is not true. Having the CEO's employment circumstances written in an agreement that foresees most eventualities is in the best interest of everyone, including the organization. A contract protects and binds both the CEO and the organization. As we review the elements of a contract, the advantages for the healthcare organization to have a contract in place become more evident.

Some organizations try to get by with a simple letter of agreement with the CEO. We think that an agreement letter is too simple for today's complex times and leaves too many issues open for interpretation, especially when litigation might be involved.

Most healthcare organizations begin the contract deliberations with the ACHE's CEO contract (see Appendix J). This document is a good starting place for negotiations, but please keep in mind that the organization *must* engage a lawyer to ensure that all technicalities are observed and that the document complies with applicable state and national laws. To merely use the sample contract without review by an attorney would be a mistake.

> A contract is a necessary tool for keeping a CEO engaged in doing what is necessary to advance the organization and to minimize his or her tendency to do nothing for fear of losing the job.

The elements of a contract are fairly straightforward and can be identified merely by reviewing the contract document. Most organizations take the tactic of developing a document that can be appended rather than spelling out all the agreement's minutia. For example, attaching a list of current benefits rather than listing each benefit in the body of the contract is a common practice. The same would be true of the job description. A contract will typically mandate an annual review, when the review is to be done, and how the review is to be conducted. We believe that spelling out these details in the contract enhances the possibility that an annual review will actually be done.

One of the clauses that protect the employer the most is the restrictive covenant, commonly known as the "covenant not to compete." This clause prevents the CEO from moving across the street to a competitor without the organization's approval. This is a tricky clause in that courts in different states interpret and enforce it differently.

According to a famous Georgia Supreme Court case, "six Philadelphia lawyers couldn't write a covenant not to compete that is enforceable in Georgia." In other states, the covenants are much more easily enforced. Be sure to keep the terms of the covenant reasonable, the geographical area covered, the job or jobs, and the types of employer. This is an important clause for the organization, so be sure it is included in your contract document.

One of the clauses we like to see included in a contract is limiting the recruitment of employees from the organization if its CEO leaves. This is a practical clause to include because CEOs often raid their former organizations for talent when they take a new assignment. This talent raid can leave the organization weak and vulnerable at a time when it is trying to recruit new leadership. Again, make sure that the clause includes a reasonable term and identifies the type of employee that cannot be recruited.

Another clause we like is one that keeps the CEO from making use of plans and documents that he or she might have been involved with while CEO of the healthcare organization. This clause would prevent the CEO from leaving and independently pursuing a deal that had been negotiated while he or she was employed by the organization.

Two parts of the contract are usually the most debated between the CEO and the board: (1) the terms of termination of the contract and (2) the amount of severance. The contract can be terminated several ways:

- by expiration;
- by the executive (by resigning or retiring);
- by death;
- by disability;
- by change in control;
- by change in duties; and
- by the organization (for cause or no cause).

Each of these methods of termination must be articulated in the contract and their wording is subject to much negotiation. The ACHE sample contract does a good job of wording these methods, but the board and the CEO should spend extra time to ensure that they are comfortable with all terms of the termination.

A severance package for the CEO should include both salary and benefits for a stated period. That period is usually no less than 12 months and could extend to 36 months. We have, on rare occasions, seen 60-month severance packages, but to us this seems excessive. The ACHE sample contract recommends 24 months. Some organizations have compromised to 12 months plus one month for each year of continuous employment up to 24 months. This seems to us a practical compromise that rewards longevity yet protects the new CEO as well. Change-of-control situations often trigger additional severance because the organization wants the CEO to do the best thing for the organization in case of a merger or acquisition. If additional severance is offered, then the

CEO will not be as concerned about his or her personal situation and work for the best outcome for the organization. A severance package of three to five years is common in these situations and, in fact, can be triggered by the CEO if circumstances warrant. Typically, a certain timeframe exists for the CEO to "pull the ripcord" on the "golden parachute."

Some organizations have opted to give salary continuance only until the CEO is re-employed. As a consideration, they will sometimes make up any difference between what the CEO previously made and his or her new salary for a period of time. Of course if the CEO increases his or her salary, this differential doesn't apply. Many healthcare organizations have opted to pay severance benefits in one lump sum immediately after termination. From a practical governance perspective, we don't think that this is such a good idea. Sometimes the organization needs information and cooperation from an exiting CEO. Having control of the severance benefit ensures that cooperation.

We have noticed several other clauses that are not always present in every contract but certainly are significant when present. First, contracts with religious organizations may include a clause that requires the CEO to comply with ethical and religious directives of the sponsoring religious body. Although this is an appropriate clause by an organization sponsored by a religious group, the CEO who agrees to the clause should be comfortable with the expectation that he or she will have to make decisions based on religious influence. Second, we have learned of a clause that requires the CEO to pay for the organization's legal costs if the CEO loses in a terms-of-contract litigation. This seems to be an especially onerous clause, and we would recommend binding arbitration as a fairer and more appropriate way to deal with conflict resolution.

A CEO contract is a responsible way for a board to define its obligations to the CEO and for the CEO to define his or her obligations to the organization. Although the contract should anticipate as many scenarios as possible, in the end, it cannot cover every eventuality. Therefore, a contract needs to be renegotiated periodically as circumstances change and new eventualities reveal themselves. A typical contract would last from three to five years and be renegotiated immediately before the final year of the contract. Some boards who have extreme confidence in their CEOs have given "evergreen" contracts that perpetually renew on each anniversary date. We really have no opinion on whether an "evergreen" contract is good or bad. We do believe, however, that from a practical governance perspective, each party should periodically take the contract out of the files and read it. Upon a new reading of the contract, everyone is often surprised at what was previously agreed to when circumstances were different.

> One of the ways to avoid the hassle of searching for a new CEO is to have the successor already identified and groomed to take over when the CEO steps aside.

CEO SUCCESSION PLANNING

CEO turnover is alive and well in healthcare; in 1999, CEO turnover averaged 10.6 percent. In some cases, CEOs leave their positions for greener pastures. Others who remember the "good old days" leave the profession altogether, frustrated or burnt out. Still others leave at the board's request because of its perceived need for new leadership. Occasionally, some retire. Whatever the reason for a CEO's departure, the end result is a disruption in management continuity.

One of the ways to avoid the hassle of searching for a new CEO is to have the successor already identified and groomed to take over when the CEO steps aside. In the ideal scenario, the old CEO steps aside, the new CEO takes the reins, and everything moves merrily along with no break in the continuity of purpose or results. Unfortunately, the ideal scenario very rarely is met because too many variables are present in today's healthcare world for the scenario to always work out perfectly. Nevertheless, just because something is complicated doesn't mean that it shouldn't be tried.

One purpose of the board is to ensure the continuation of the enterprise and minimization of disruption through succession planning.

When should succession planning begin? In a 1999 *Harvard Business Review* article, "Changing Leaders: The Board's Role in CEO Succession," Alfred M. Zeien, retired chair and CEO of Gillette Company, recommended that succession planning should begin four years before the chief executive is expected to step down. Considering that many hospital CEOs only stay in their positions for about five years, heeding Zeien's advice would mean that within a year or so of hiring the CEO, the board must start succession planning. Also, unlike in many *Fortune* 500 companies where CEOs often announce how long they plan to stay in the organization immediately after being hired, this practice is not common in most healthcare organizations. Many healthcare organizations do groom an individual within the organization to assume the reins of the CEO should the CEO step aside, retire, or leave. The individual groomed is looked upon as the "number two" in the organization and is sought out in the absence of the CEO. Twenty years ago, this individual normally would have been the chief operating officer. Nowadays, this individual could also be the chief financial officer or the chief nursing officer. Interestingly, the succession planning responsibility can be successfully discharged by informally designating someone in another organization as the future replacement of the CEO. Often, this is evidenced by someone who worked in the organization and is currently working somewhere else, gathering the experience to return as the CEO.

The board's role in succession planning breaks down into several tasks. First, the board should make certain that succession planning is being done by bringing it to the attention of the CEO and adding it on the CEO's annual performance appraisal objectives. Even the most reluctant CEO will begin planning if he or she knows that a serious discussion will take place annually on what efforts have been made toward that goal.

Second, the board should sign off on any designation of the heir(s) apparent or any succession planning efforts. The board should adopt the succession plan as its plan and not just the CEO's. The board should accept that this is a joint duty and not one totally delegated without supervision to the CEO. In the same *Harvard Business Review* article, George D. Kennedy, former chair and CEO of International Minerals and Chemical Corporation and of the Mallinckrodt Group, emphasized that the board and the CEO have to remember that they have different roles in the process: "The CEO is the point person in the entire succession process; there's no question about that. But the CEO needs to understand that the board is going to make the ultimate decision on who the next CEO will be."

Third, the board should make sure that any promises it has made are communicated to the succeeding board leadership. In fact, if promises were or need to be made, the current and succeeding board should adhere to them. In general, the board should limit itself to as few promises as possible.

This now brings us to the problems of succession planning, given that succession planning inevitably is fraught with problems. A review of some of the most obvious problems will give you a good idea of what a board is up against when it signs off on succession plans.

Succession plans make assumptions and, in a fast-changing environment, assumptions can change quickly. The organization that was a freestanding facility last month may decide this month to join a system or to create a system on its own. The former "number two" and heir apparent may be passed over as CEO-designate as part of a bargaining position or in deference to "perceived equity" with the other entity. When the succession plan was first designed, no one foresaw the possibilities of the combination and therefore the plan was rendered inoperative.

Boards change. A change in board membership or board chair can mean change in how a succession plan should be implemented. A new board chair may look at the internal candidates differently and be unwilling to be held to the promises of the previous board chair. Promises of this nature tend not to be in writing.

The heir apparent may not be ready to succeed the CEO. This can come about through failures on the heir's part or because designating a formal heir may be the equivalent of placing a target on the heir's back. Issues that deal with the CEO can now be readily placed on the head of the heir apparent and the heir becomes the target for ill will really meant for the departed CEO.

Designating an heir apparent may cause others in the organization, who might be well qualified by the time the CEO steps aside, to leave. Because of this, some organizations might indicate to several executives that they are being considered as CEO replacements. The question then becomes whether the replacements can continue to act as supportive team members for each other in an environment that only picks one winner at the end.

If the board tries succession planning and it fails, the board and the organization have a few alternatives that will give them breathing room until a new CEO is named. Numerous organizations have found going outside the organization to look for the new CEO beneficial because either internal candidates are not deemed adequate, or a change in direction or philosophy is called for, or no one internally wants the job. Sometimes an outside search is conducted even when an excellent candidate exists internally because the board wants to make sure that the new CEO

Numerous organizations have found going outside the organization to look for the new CEO beneficial because either internal candidates are not deemed adequate, or a change in direction or philosophy is called for, or no one internally wants the job.

is the very best that was available at the time. The outside search validates the selection of the internal candidate because he or she would have beaten the very best available to get the position.

To minimize the disruption created when the CEO departs unexpectedly, an internal individual can be designated as the "acting CEO." Typically, the acting CEO is the leading candidate for the job. Sometimes, however, the board decides to bring in an interim CEO whose sole job is to hold things together until a new CEO is appointed. With someone in the CEO's chair, decisions can be made that allow the organization to move forward while the search continues.

Finally, we know for a fact that succession plans are possible and that an increasing number of organizations have such plans today (see Appendix K for a sample CEO succession planning process from Memorial Health System). We think you will find that it "cuts to the chase" and both clarifies and sets in motion a much-needed activity.

13

Strategic Planning and Crisis Management

STRATEGIC PLANNING

Strategic planning has long been an implicit responsibility of the board. Ironically, it remains one of the more difficult tasks for the board to perform effectively. Several issues compound the process. First, although some board members have participated in strategic planning in their professional lives, still others are unfamiliar with what it is all about. Second, the board has a lot to contend with today, given the rapid changes of the healthcare landscape and the complexities of running a healthcare organization. Numerous books and articles have been written on strategic planning, and we don't attempt to cover those concepts here. Instead, we simply share what we believe is a useful framework to consider for those unfamiliar with strategic planning.

Purpose

A strategic plan should chart a course for your organization over the next three to five years. Healthcare organizations are finding increasingly that three-year planning horizons are the preferred option because of how quickly the environment is changing.

Considerations

The strategic plan developed should:

The goals in the plan should be limited to goals that, if achieved, will have a significant, positive impact on the organization.

- be consistent with the organization's vision, mission, and values.
- be strategic rather than tactical.
- take into consideration the organization's strengths, weaknesses, opportunities, and threats (commonly referred to as a SWOT analysis).
- provide clear direction to staff who will be charged with implementing the plan.
- not attempt to be all-inclusive. In other words, the goals in the plan should be limited to those four to six goals, for example, that, if achieved, will have a significant positive impact on the organization.

Information gathering is best if it involves gathering information about the external environment (national and regional trends); the local marketplace (competitor analysis); and organizational performance data (financial, clinical quality, public perception, etc.).

Strategic planning should be process-driven and outcome-oriented and driven by the strategic planning committee. (Strategic planning committees are often composed of the entire board; a subset of the board; a board management team; or a team comprising board members, subsidiary board members, and management staff.)

Phase I: Gathering Information

Whether you engage an outside strategic planning consultant or have staff perform the legwork, the information-gathering phase is extremely important. Planning for the future is difficult unless you have a clear sense of where the organization stands today. Information gathering is best if it involves gathering information about the external environment (national and regional trends); the local marketplace (competitor analysis); and organizational performance data (financial, clinical quality, public perception, etc.).

Phase II: Identifying Critical Issues

Based on the information gathered and other observations, the strategic planning committee can start crystallizing the issues to be addressed in the strategic plan. It should be a process that begins with presenting all potential issues and then winnowing them down to the four to six key challenges that the organization is likely to face over the next several years.

Phase III: Developing Goals and Strategies

Once the key challenges have been identified, additional legwork is generally required. In other words, once you know the challenges, you need to lay out the attendant issues so that appropriate goals and strategies can be developed. To this end, we recommend the preparation of issue briefings, which is much like those we recommended in Chapter 7 for issues under committee consideration. The issue briefings should identify the challenges; include relevant background information; and provide options, and their likely financial implications, for addressing the challenges. If members of the management team do not sit on the strategic planning committee, we recommend that they be integrated in some way into the process at this point. Management's view and the board's view of strategic challenge may ultimately differ, but the strategic planning committee must have an opportunity to consider management's perspective. (Quite often, the task of preparing such issue briefings is delegated to staff members who have at their disposal the organizational knowledge needed to provide background information and a firsthand understanding of realistic options for addressing the challenges.)

Phase IV: Putting the Plan Together

At this juncture, we have observed that the strategic planning process could suddenly go awry, which may be caused simply by confusion about what level of detail should be included in the plan. We believe that the strategic plan should contain only the following elements, which are defined in Exhibit 13.1:

1. vision and mission statements;
2. summary of environmental analyses and implications;
3. four to six strategic goals; and
4. macro strategies for achieving those goals.

Exhibit 13.1: Definition of Stategic Plan Elements

1. *Vision statement*—a succinct statement of the organization's desired future state.
2. *Mission statement*—a brief discussion of how the organization intends to fulfill its vision.
3. *Strategic goals*—broad statements that articulate what the organization needs to do to survive and thrive.
4. *Macro strategies*—broad statements that articulate how the organization plans to operationalize the plan's goals.

The strategic plan is not the place for tactical detail or specific objectives—those belong in the staff-developed, annual action plan. It is the juncture, however, for considering the financial ramifications of any goals under consideration.

Interestingly, many healthcare organizations have a two-track process: (1) the three-year strategic plan and (2) an action plan that guides staff's day-to-day work. Often, the two documents are largely unrelated. Worse yet, the strategic plan is dusted off by staff before a board meeting when they must provide a progress report on goal attainment. They do so by figuring out how to take what they were doing, absent of strategic plan directives, and make that activity sound like it was an outgrowth of the strategic plan. A related problem is when the strategic plan was developed apart from the organization's budget, so the goals as stated would "break the bank" if they were implemented as intended.

But another way is possible. If the strategic planning committee develops the strategic plan, pays close attention to its impact on the budget process, and then hands it over to management to use in the development of an annual action plan, the interrelationship between the two documents won't be artificial or unrealistic. In other words, the strategic plan can, and should, drive the development of the annual action plan.

A benefit of the annual action plan, besides the fact that it gives management a role in charting the organization's future directions, is that it covers a relatively short time frame. Whereas a strategic plan may have a three- or even five-year horizon, an annual action plan can be much more responsive to marketplace and organization changes. Critical elements of the action plan are the delineation of quantifiable objectives for achieving strategic plan goals and strategies, timelines for completion, and accountabilities for their achievement.

The board's responsibility as it relates to strategic planning does not end with the plan's development. The document should be discussed periodically at board meetings to gauge whether new circumstances require any goal modification. In addition, the plan can be quite useful in helping the board stay on course. In other words, to a large extent, action considered by the board should be consistent with the plan's objectives. If an issue that seems to diverge from the plan is presented to the board, the board, at the very least, should be able to defend why the issue, though seemingly unrelated to the organization's strategic course, merits discussion.

The strategic plan can, and should, drive the development of the annual action plan.

Whereas a strategic plan may have a three- or even five-year horizon, an annual action plan can be much more responsive to marketplace and organization changes.

CRISIS MANAGEMENT

Two reasons that crises become crises are (1) that no steps to prevent them from escalating have been taken and (2) that the responses by the organization and the board are often inconsistent at best and often disastrous.

One of the truest tests of a board's effectiveness is how it handles a crisis. Fortunately, full-blown crises are not something with which the vast majority of boards must contend. That said, two reasons that crises become crises are (1) that no steps to prevent them from escalating have been taken and (2) that the responses by the organization and the board are often inconsistent at best and often disastrous. Crises that boards may face can be those that result from:

- an organizational failing (e.g., the sudden public disclosure that the organization is in financial peril or is the subject of a federal investigation);
- an alleged medical blunder (e.g., the death of a patient because of a medication error);
- the alleged ethical or criminal wrongdoing of a senior executive or board member as an agent of the organization; or
- personal scandal related to a staff or board member.

In any of these cases, the board's role is, first and foremost, to be cognizant and compliant with the organization's policy for handling such crises. (If an organization does not have a crisis-management policy, then the board may wish to communicate that the development of such a policy is an expectation.) Most board members, we hope, are introduced to the organization's crisis-management plan during the board orientation. These plans typically delineate the policy for handling various types of crisis situations, including the procedure for notifying the board and staff of the crisis; the official "crisis spokesperson" of the organization; and the plan for keeping affected individuals and the media apprised of the situation. As agents of the organization, the board, when faced with a crisis, must strike a balance among being forthcoming with information, not breaching confidences, and doing its part to assist the organization in getting beyond the crisis.

The tired cliché "loose lips sink ships" is the one common mistake board members make during a crisis. Often, because the board members are community leaders, they have many business and personal contacts who want the "inside story" on the situation. With no malice or forethought, and actually quite the opposite, the board member willingly offers to those who ask his or her take on the situation. Though well intentioned, comments made during casual conversation frequently come back to haunt the board member and the entire organization. Many board members have been rather unpleasantly surprised to see their casual comments appear in print only a short time later.

Any public comments should be made by a single representative of the organization— ideally the CEO.

In our opinion, we believe any public comments should be made by a single representative of the organization—ideally the CEO. Although some would argue that the spokesperson should instead be the board chair, we don't agree. Keep in mind that what makes news tends to be the "ugly" part of the story. The board chair, while eminently qualified to lead the board, may not have much experience talking to the media. CEOs, though not always adept at it, are likely to have somewhat more experience. The board chair should not be anxious to take on the media in troubled times, but certainly should have part of the spotlight, at least when good news can be shared.

Even the suggestion of trouble can quickly escalate to unmanageable proportions, so board denial of the crisis is certainly not a viable solution.

Certainly, another natural tendency in times of crisis—particularly if the crisis is financial or alleged organizational wrongdoing—is to hope that by doing nothing the furor will die down. Unfortunately, over the past few years, the media have made clear that such wishful thinking is just that. Keep in mind that although in the past decades healthcare organizations were trusted and often were revered community institutions, public confidence in the entire healthcare industry is perhaps at an all-time low today. Even the suggestion of trouble can quickly escalate to unmanageable proportions, so board denial of the crisis is certainly not a viable solution.

Action-oriented boards may not always be able to prevent crises from unfolding, but they can send a powerful message—the organization is prepared to deal with the crisis and not be undone by it. How can the board send that message if it leaves the talking to the CEO? It sends that message by pulling together to address the situation head-on. What board members do in the boardroom in times of crisis is critical to how the crisis will play out. Board members in crisis must put aside their differences and provide the CEO and the organization with the support they need to right the ship.

14

The Board and the Community

THE LAST TWO chapters have focused on two very specific and high-stakes board responsibilities. In this chapter, we will discuss in some detail the board's responsibility to the community. Regardless of hospital or system ownership, serving the community is an organization's *raison d'être*. Generating a shareholder return, even for investor-owned organizations from whom a return is expected, is virtually impossible if community needs are unmet.

Clearly, the challenge of meeting community needs has been compounded over the years by the social ills that contribute to "unhealthy communities." The number of underinsured and uninsured is growing, and communities also combat mounting health crises related to drug use, violence, and other health problems attributable, at least in part, to poverty. So the challenge today is not simply to provide a certain amount of uncompensated care, but for organizations to do their part in building healthier communities.

In recent years, the media have called attention to for-profit and not-for-profit organizations that, at least in the public's eye, have not lived up to this obligation. We've heard about organizations that failed to do their share to treat the underinsured and uninsured. We've heard about organizations that spent millions of dollars in building new structures but have not been involved

> The challenge today is not simply to provide a certain amount of uncompensated care, but for organizations to do their part in building healthier communities.

in building healthier communities. These stories are prevalent, and they are not pretty.

In some cases, the bad rap that some organizations have gotten and are getting is deserved. In many cases, however, we believe that some of the bad press is instead a result of misinformation or lack of communication about all the good that organizations do on behalf of their communities.

Recent evidence suggests that boards are increasingly recognizing that the community as a whole is among its most important customer.

Faced with declining profitability and the related challenge of doing more with less, serving the community is admittedly a more difficult proposition. Nevertheless, neither the board nor the organization can afford to let this priority fall off the list. In fact, recent evidence suggests that boards are increasingly recognizing that the community as a whole is among its most important customers.

As we selected our interviewees for this book, we identified CEOs and organizations that are known for being leaders in the field. We did not specifically look for those whose organizations are leaders in meeting community needs. Nevertheless, we were pleased to learn that six of our CEO interviewees work for organizations that are highlighted in "Motivating Community Health Through Hospital Board, CEO, and Organizational Performance Evaluations," a study conducted by the American College of Healthcare Executives with funding from the W. K. Kellogg Foundation.

In Chapter 10, we talked about the growing trend toward tying CEO compensation to community health improvement. In this chapter, our focus is on the methods some organizations employ for making community health improvement a priority. For Mission Hospital Regional Medical Center, improving community health speaks to the system's and hospital's mission.

As a member of St. Joseph Health System, Mission Hospital commits 10 percent of its net income toward programs that benefit the medically underserved. In addition, 1 percent of its operating expenses are designated for programs that contribute to healthy community activities including a family resource center, community health education programs, and a "helping hands" program that provides clothing and other essentials to needy patients. In 1998, the hospital contributed $9.7 million to support these and other initiatives to meet community needs.

Obviously, both the system board and the hospital board are integral to Mission Hospital's ability and willingness to make such a substantive commitment to the community. Without the board's full support, even the most committed CEO would be hard pressed to gain support for this type of multifaceted program of community support.

We believe that many hospitals and systems throughout the United States are making similar commitments to their communities; but in some cases, the word just does not get out. In our view, letting the community know that you care and are working on its behalf is not inappropriate; in fact, we encourage you to do just that. Mission Hospital sends this message in its *Annual Report of Community Benefits.* The publication details St. Joseph's and Mission Hospital's philosophy on community service, as well as identifies the specific programs they were involved in and the funds allocated to them.

Just as Peter Bastone, Mission Hospital's CEO, has his board's full support for the hospital's charitable activities, so too does Philip Newbold, CEO of Memorial Health System. Memorial Health System has been recognized nationwide for its community service and was a recipient of the AHA's "Living the Vision" award in 1999. The award honors individuals and organizations that carry out the AHA's vision of a society of healthy communities where all individuals reach their highest health potential.

Memorial Health System is well known for its "community plunges" whereby board members, senior hospital executives, and medical staff leaders join civic leaders to address such issues

> Letting the community know that you care and are working on its behalf is not inappropriate; in fact, we encourage you to do just that.

as violence, homelessness, and teen pregnancy. Memorial Health System has also developed other approaches to improving community health. As part of its Community Health Partnership, for example, the system provides up to two years of free health coverage to qualified uninsured families enrolled in the program.

Obviously, helping the community requires dollars, and dollars may be increasingly difficult to come by for hospitals and systems alike. At Memorial Health System, the funds for community initiatives are made available through an annual tithing. Tithing is not a new concept, but it is one that may be unfamiliar to some board members.

Memorial Health System's board-approved tithing policy calls for allocating 10 percent of the system's bottom line annually to address community health issues. The system's 1998 tithing was more than $3.5 million. Newbold pointed out that the tithing policy is a *policy*; it doesn't fall prey to other budgetary concerns and cannot be dismissed at will. That said, the magic number, Newbold said, does not need to be 10 percent; it could be 8 or 5 percent. He also pointed out that at Memorial Health System, the money invested in its community in 1999 comes from its 1998 earnings. The key to making tithing work is to establish a policy and then, with the board's guidance, determine how best to spend the funds.

If you are a CEO or a board member in an organization where improving community health is not an ongoing priority, we would be surprised. Our guess is that hospitals or systems that do not follow this responsibility are no longer in business. Still, taking stock periodically of what you are doing for the community and what you still need to do is worthwhile. Exhibit 14.1 presents suggestions on how boards can get involved in improving community health. These suggestions were adapted from *The Trustee Handbook for Health Care Governance* by James E. Orlikoff and Mary K. Totten.

The key to making tithing work is to establish a policy and then, with the board's guidance, determine how best to spend the funds.

Exhibit 14.1: Seven Ways to Get Involved in Community Health Improvement

1. Get to know the community your organization serves. Where is it located? Who lives there—get to know age, gender, ethnicity, religion, etc.? What specific health issues/concerns do they have?
2. Partner with care and resource providers in the community. You can learn a lot about the community's needs when you work with these groups.
3. Establish vision, values, and plans with your partners to ensure you are all working toward the same goals.
4. Create health status indicators. Share this information regularly with your partners and board.
5. Establish annual health improvement goals based on the health status indicators you developed. Measure your organization's progress and performance against these goals.
6. Incorporate community health improvement in the CEO's evaluation criteria.
7. Ask the board to evaluate community health improvement as part of its self-evaluation process.

Source: Adapted from J. E. Orlikoff and M. K. Totten. 1998. *The Trustee Handbook for Health Care Governance.* Chicago: American Hospital Publishing, Inc.

15

What the Future Holds

"Hospital Prices Jump"

"Hospitals Want More Money from Congress"

"Getting Squeezed: Hospitals Complain That Managed Care Puts Them in a Financial Vise by Delaying Payments"

"Report Predicts Huge HIPAA Price Tag"

"Hospital Physician Group in Maryland Bankrupt"

"Shattered Image: Fraud Convictions Haunt the Healthcare Industry As It Seeks More Medicare Money"

"Bitter Pills—The Often Frustrating Way to Control Escalating Drug Costs"

"Another Hospital System Unloading Unprofitable HMO"

"Healthcare Groups Split on Mandatory Mistake Reporting"

YOU HAVE JUST read headlines found in recent issues of *Modern Healthcare* magazine. They give you a pretty good idea of what the future—at least the immediate future—holds for CEOs and their boards. At the risk of oversimplifying things, we believe that over the next few years, leaders of hospitals and systems nationwide, regardless of size and ownership, will likely be charged with leading the way in:

As the impact of the infamous Balanced Budget Act intensifies, boards will be challenged to find ways to create viable new sources of revenue.

1. *identifying and implementing revenue-enhancement strategies.* Even in the best of times, hospital boards concern themselves with the organization's finances. As the impact of the infamous Balanced Budget Act intensifies, boards will be challenged to find ways to create viable new sources of revenue.

2. *divesting unprofitable businesses or product lines.* A decade ago, the race was on to sign contracts with a multitude of managed care plans, as well as develop hospital-owned plans. Well, the flower is off the bloom. This "sure-fire" strategy has proven disappointing for many hospitals. As a result, governing boards will be faced with leading their organizations in the painful process of cutting their losses.

The seemingly unabating nursing shortage is an issue to hospitals nationwide. As boards well know, compromising quality of care is not the solution. Finding an appropriate solution to this shortage will keep many boards busy in the months to come.

3. *coping with labor shortages.* The downside of a healthy economy is that finding qualified employees is no small feat. With unemployment at its lowest level in decades, organizations are challenged to retain qualified employees and attract others who are capable and qualified. Hospitals are like all other businesses in this regard, except they face an additional shortage of serious concern. The seemingly unabating nursing shortage is an issue to hospitals nationwide. As boards well know, compromising quality of care is not the solution. Finding an appropriate solution to this shortage will keep many boards busy in the months to come.

4. *rethinking the organization's hospital-physician "bonding" strategy.* Just as the promise of managed care participation has not materialized, neither has the promise of hospital-owned physician practices. So boards now must not only think about unloading unprofitable practices but

consider yet another approach for creating strong hospital-physician partnerships.

5. *disintegrating the integrated organization.* 1999 was certainly a year when the experts who told us what the future would look like were eating their words. First, managed care. Then, physician practices. Now, integrated delivery. It's not working as planned. CEOs and boards that spent months on developing complex integration strategies are now back at the drawing board asking "What's wrong with this picture?" We are betting that "disintegration" will be the buzzword of the next few years and an equally daunting, albeit important, priority for boards everywhere.

We are betting that "disintegration" will be the buzzword of the next few years and an equally daunting, albeit important, priority for boards everywhere.

6. *demonstrating the quality of medical care.* The Institute of Medicine's report on medical errors may ultimately have regulatory implications for providers. Even if that is not the case, the public is sufficiently concerned about medical mistakes to compel hospitals to address the issue on their own. Boards that believe this is simply a public-relations issue caused by bad press may be in for a surprise. Quality assurance matters have always been high on the board's agenda; but at least for the immediate future, they are likely to become an even higher priority.

7. *mastering the intricacies of Medicare and HIPAA compliance.* By this point, the government's seriousness about stemming Medicare fraud and abuse should be pretty obvious. Hospital CEOs and boards that aren't making every reasonable effort to make sure they are playing by the rules may get their infamous 15 minutes of fame in the near future. HIPAA compliance is no less daunting an issue.

8. *understanding the implications of E-Health.* No one would argue that the Internet already has a profound impact on all aspects of life, including healthcare purchasing and delivery. Anticipating the impact of E-Health at the

organizational level is among the more challenging tasks that boards and CEOs will face. The upside of the technological revolution for boards is that they too can harness the power of information technology to become more informed board members.

The eight issues cited above are likely just the tip of the iceberg. In other words, another eight issues likely will command the board's attention and require innovative leadership in the next few years. Also, given the frenetic pace of change in the healthcare marketplace, by the time boards successfully address these issues, they will face an equally daunting set of new issues.

NO PAIN, NO GAIN

Healthcare governance is clearly one of those bad news, good news propositions. The bad news is that governing effectively has never been more difficult than it is today. As a result, the level of board member commitment required is greater than ever. And, the decisions boards face that can make or break the organization are plentiful.

Now the good news. Not unlike athletes who train for years, participate in grueling events like triathlons, and cross the finish line looking exhausted but triumphant, board members can feel similar exhilaration for a job well done. Practical governance can indeed be a painful process; but for those who are willing to become "students" of governance and continue to learn about what makes them an effective member of the team and be a meaningful contributor to the board, the rewards can be great.

There is more good news. Our interviews confirmed that there are plenty of healthcare CEOs who understand their role and understand yours very well. They are grateful for your leadership and are committed to providing you with the education and resources you need to do your job well. We also believe that the

> The upside of the technological revolution for boards is that they too can harness the power of information technology to become more informed board members.

> Practical governance can indeed be a painful process; but for those who are willing to become "students" of governance and continue to learn about what makes them an effective member of the team and be a meaningful contributor to the board, the rewards can be great.

caliber of current board chairs is better than ever. These individuals have demonstrated a long-term commitment to the organizations that they serve, as evidenced by their years of service before assuming the position of chair. These individuals deserve your admiration and are, for the most part, worthy of emulation.

In the final analysis, practical governance is both an art and a science. You may have vision. You may have a vast repository of useful knowledge. You may have great people skills. That's a start. But even the "best and the brightest" do not have the luxury of governing by instinct. To truly be the best you can be, you must augment your innate abilities with a solid foundation of understanding what constitutes practical governance. Your organization is counting on you.

Appendix A:
Selected Resources for Healthcare
CEOs and Boards

ARTICLES

Bilchik, G. S. 1999. "Outside/In: Health Care Boards Look Beyond Their Communities for Trustees." *Trustee* 52 (7).

Conger, J. A., D. Finegold, and E. E. Lawler. 1998. "Appraising Boardroom Performance." *Harvard Business Review* 78 (1).

Ferry, R. M. 1999. "Boardrooms Yesterday, Today, and Tomorrow." *Chief Executive* 142 (i).

Lorsch, J. W., and R. Khurana. 1999. "Changing Leaders: The Board's Role in CEO Succession." A Roundtable with Philip Caldwell, George D. Kennedy, G. G. Michelson, Henry Wendt, and Alfred M. Zeien. *Harvard Business Review* 79 (3).

McFarlan, F. W. 1999. "Working on Nonprofit Boards: Don't Assume the Shoe Fits." *Harvard Business Review* 77 (6).

National Center for NonProfit Boards. 1999. "Boards in Motion: How to Have Better Meetings." *Board Member* 8 (8).

BOOKS

Carver, J. 1997. *Boards That Make a Difference, Second Edition.* San Francisco: Jossey-Bass Publishers.

Griffith, J. R. 1999. *The Well-Managed Healthcare Organization, Fourth Edition.* Chicago: Health Administration Press.

Orlikoff, J. E., and M. K. Totten. 1998. *The Trustee Handbook for Health Care Governance.* Chicago: American Hospital Publishing, Inc.

Pointer, D. D., and J. E. Orlikoff. 1999. *Board Work: Governing Health Care Organizations.* San Francisco: Jossey-Bass Publishers.

Welcome to the Board! An Orientation for the New Health Care Trustee. 1999. Chicago: Health Forum Inc., and Health Research and Educational Trust of New Jersey.

BOOKLETS, RESEARCH REPORTS, AND OTHER RESOURCES

Contracts for Healthcare Executives 2000, Fourth Edition. 2001. Chicago: American College of Healthcare Executives.

Evaluating the Performance of the Hospital CEO in a Total Quality Management Environment. 1993. Chicago: American College of Healthcare Executives.

Motivating Community Health Through Hospital Board, CEO, and Organizational Performance Evaluations. In Press. Chicago: Foundation of the American College of Healthcare Executives, American Hospital Association, and the W. K. Kellogg Foundation.

The Partnership Study: A Study of the Roles and Working Relationships of the Hospital Board Chairman, CEO, and Medical Staff President: Survey Findings. 1992. Chicago: American College of Healthcare Executives.

The Partnership Study Phase II: A Study of the Roles and Working Relationships of the Hospital Board Chairman, CEO, and Medical Staff President. 1996. Chicago: American College of Healthcare Executives, American Hospital Association, American Medical Association, and Ernst & Young LLP.

Robinson, M. K. 1994. *Developing the Nonprofit Board: Strategies for Orienting, Educating, and Motivating Board Members.* Washington, DC: National Center for Nonprofit Boards.

Shining Light on Your Board's Passage to the Future (Revised Edition). 1997. Chicago: American Hospital Association Center for Health Care Leadership and Ernst & Young LLP.

The Role of the Board Chairperson. 1992. Washington, DC: National Center for Nonprofit Boards.

SUGGESTED PERIODICAL

Trustee. The only monthly magazine specifically for board members of healthcare organizations. Published by the American Hospital Association. For more information call 800/621-6902.

SEMINARS

The following organizations offer conferences tailored for medical staff leaders, healthcare executives, and board members.

American College of Healthcare Executives Partnership Institute, Chicago, Illinois. For more information call 312/424-9300.

The Estes Park Institute, Englewood, Colorado. For more information call 800/223-4430.

The Governance Institute, La Jolla, California. For more information call 858/551-0144.

WEB SITES

American College of Healthcare Executives at *www.ache.org*.

The Estes Park Institute at *www.estespark.org*.

The Governance Institute at *www.governanceinstitute.com*.

National Center for Nonprofit Boards at *www.ncnb.org*.

Appendix B:
Sample Board Meeting Agenda

MEMORIAL HEALTH SYSTEM
BOARD OF DIRECTORS
ANNUAL MEETING

Wednesday, March 31, 1999
7:30 am - Epworth Room

AGENDA

Person Responsible

I. Call to Order

II. Mini Education Session

III. Recognition of Retiring Directors

IV. Approve Minutes from the
November 25, 1998 Board Meeting

V. Chairman's Report

VI. CEO's Report

VII. COO's Report
    A. Hospital Quality Report
    B. System Quality Report

VIII. Board Committee Reports
    A. Finance Committee
    B. Audit Committee
    C. Investment Committee
    D. Nominating/Bylaws Committee
        1. Election of Hospital Trustees and Officers, Memorial Health System Directors and Officers, and Omega Directors and Officers
        2. Re-approval of the MHS Bylaws (Joint Commission Requirement - every 3 years)
    E. Compensation Committee

IX. Other Business
    A. Next Board Meeting: As a reminder, the June meeting is a combined meeting with the Executive Committee and is scheduled June 17 at LaPorte Medical Group - 7:30 am.
    B. Board Recognition Dinner: Sunday, April 25, 1999 - Carriage House beginning at 6:00 pm invitations forthcoming.
    C. Next Community Plunge: Wednesday, June 23 from 12:00-5:00 pm. Theme: Gang Violence.

X. Adjournment

Source: Adapted with permission of Memorial Health System. 1999. South Bend, Indiana.

Appendix C:
Sample Conflict-of-Interest Policy

ARTICLE I: *Purpose*

The purpose of the conflicts of interest policy is to protect the Corporation's interest when it is contemplating entering into a transaction or arrangement that might benefit the private interest of an officer or director of the Corporation. This policy is intended to supplement but not replace any applicable state laws governing conflicts of interest applicable to nonprofit and charitable corporations.

ARTICLE II: *Definitions*

1.   Interested Person

Any director, principal officer, or member of a committee with board-delegated powers who has direct or indirect financial interest, as defined below, is an interested person. If a person is an interested person with respect to any entity in the health care system of which the Corporation is a part, he or she is an interested person with respect to all entities in the health care system.

2. Financial Interest

A person has a financial interest if the person has, directly or indirectly, through business, investment or family —

   a. an ownership or investment interest in any entity with which the Corporation has a transaction or arrangement, or
   b. a compensation arrangement with the Corporation or with any entity or individual with which the Corporation has a transaction or arrangement, or
   c. a potential ownership or investment interest in, or compensation arrangement with, any entity or individual with which the Corporation is negotiating a transaction or arrangement.

Compensation includes direct and indirect remuneration as well as gifts or favors that are substantial in nature.

A financial interest is not necessarily a conflict of interest. Under Article III, Section 2, a person who has a financial interest may have a conflict of interest only if the appropriate board or committee decides that a conflict of interest exists.

ARTICLE III: *Procedures*

1. Duty to Disclose

In connection with any actual or possible conflicts of interest, an interested person must disclose the existence of his or her financial interest and must be given the opportunity to disclose all material facts to the directors and members of committees with board-delegated powers considering the proposed transaction or arrangement.

2. Determining Whether a Conflict of Interest Exists

After disclosure of the financial interest and all material facts, and after any discussion with the board or committee, the interested person shall leave the board or committee meeting while the determination of a conflict of interest is discussed and voted upon. The remaining board or committee members shall decide if a conflict of interest exists.

3. Procedures for Addressing the Conflict of Interest

   a. An interested person may make a presentation at the board or committee meeting, but after such presentation, he/she shall leave the meeting during the discussion of, and the vote on, the transaction or arrangement that results in the conflict of interest.
   b. The chairperson of the board or committee shall, if appropriate, appoint a disinterested person or committee to investigate alternatives to the proposed transaction or arrangement.
   c. After exercising due diligence, the board or committee shall determine whether the Corporation can obtain a more advantageous transaction or arrangement with reasonable efforts from a person or entity that would not give rise to a conflict of interest.
   d. If a more advantageous transaction or arrangement is not reasonably attainable under circumstances that would not give rise to a conflict of interest, the board or committee shall determine by a majority vote of the disinterested directors whether the transaction or arrangement is in the Corporation's best interest and for its own benefit and whether the transaction is fair and reasonable to the Corporation and shall make its

decision as to whether to enter into the transaction or arrangement in conformity with such determination.

4. Violations of the Conflict of Interest Policy

    a. If the board or committee has reasonable cause to believe that a member has failed to disclose actual or possible conflicts of interest, it shall inform the member of the basis for such belief and afford the member an opportunity to explain the alleged failure to disclose.

    b. If, after hearing the response of the member and making such further investigation as may be warranted in the circumstances, the board or committee determines that the member has in fact failed to disclose an actual or possible conflict of interest, it shall take appropriate disciplinary and corrective action.

ARTICLE IV: *Records of Proceedings*

The minutes of the board and all committee with board-delegated powers shall contain—

    1. The names of the persons who disclosed or otherwise were found to have a financial interest in connection with an actual or possible conflict of interest, the nature of the financial interest, any action taken to determine whether a conflict of interest was present, and the board's or committee's decision as to whether a conflict of interest in fact existed.

    2. The names of the persons who were present for discussions and votes relating to the transaction or

arrangement, the content of the discussion, including any alternatives to the proposed transaction or arrangement, and a record of any votes taken in connection therewith.

ARTICLE V: *Compensation*

1. A voting member of the board of directors who receives compensation, directly or indirectly, from the Corporation for services is precluded from voting on matters pertaining to that member's compensation.
2. A physician who is a voting member of the board of directors and receives compensation, directly or indirectly, from the Corporation for services is precluded from discussing and voting on matters pertaining to that member's and other physician's compensation. No physician or physician director, either individually or collectively, is prohibited from providing information to the board of directors regarding physician compensation.
3. A voting member of any committee whose jurisdiction includes compensation matters and who receives compensation, directly or indirectly, from the Corporation for services is precluded from voting on matters pertaining to that member's compensation.
4. Physician who receive compensation, directly, or indirectly, from the Corporation, whether as employees or independent contractors, are precluded from membership on any committee whose jurisdiction includes compensation matters. No physician, either individually or collectively, is prohibited from providing information to any committee regarding physician compensation.

ARTICLE VI: *Annual Statements*

Each director, principal officer and member of a committee with board-delegated powers shall annually sign a statement which affirms that such person—

    a. has received a copy of the conflicts of interest policy,
    b. has read and understands the policy,
    c. has agreed to comply with the policy, and
    d. understands that the Corporation is a charitable organization and that in order to maintain its federal tax exemption it must engage primarily in activities which accomplish one or more or its tax-exempt purposes.

ARTICLE VII: *Periodic Reviews*

To ensure that the Corporation operates in a manner consistent with its charitable purposes and that it does not engage in activities that could jeorpardize its status as an organization exempt from federal income tax, periodic reviews shall be conducted. The periodic reviews shall, at a minimum, include the following subjects:

    a. Whether compensation arrangements and benefits are reasonable and are the result of arm's-length bargaining.
    b. Whether acquisitions of physicians practices and other provider services result in inurement or impermissible private benefit.
    c. Whether partnership and joint venture arrangements and arrangements with management service organizations and physician hospital organizations conform to written policies, are properly recorded, reflect

reasonable payments for goods and services, further
the Corporation's charitable purposes and do not
result in inurement or impermissible private benefit.

d. Whether agreements to provide health care and
agreements with other health care providers, employees, and third-party payors further the Corporation's
charitable purposes and do not result in inurement
or impermissible private benefit.

ARTICLE VIII: *Use of Outside Experts*

In conducting the periodic reviews provided for in Article VII,
the Corporation may, but need not, use outside advisors. If outside experts are used their use shall not relieve the board of its
responsibility for ensuring that periodic reviews are conducted.

Source: Courtesy of the Health Care Practice Group of the law
firm of King & Spalding. Atlanta, Georgia.
Note: Conflicts Policy recommended by the IRS for tax exempt
organizations.

Appendix D:
Sample Board Member
Responsibilities

CHAIR/PRESIDENT OF THE BOARD

- Chairs board and executive committee meetings
- Serves as ex-officio member of all board committees and attend meetings when invited
- Appoints all committee chairs and, with the chief executive, recommends who will serve on committees
- Identifies committee recommendations that should be presented to the full board
- Assists chief executive in preparing agenda for board meetings
- Conducts periodic board member assessments with chief executive
- Conducts chief executive's annual performance evaluation
- Oversees search for new chief executive
- Negotiates compensation and benefits of chief executive
- Works with nominating committee to recruit new board members

- Assists chief executive in conducting new board member orientation
- Monitors financial planning and financial reporting
- Serves as chief volunteer of the organization (nonprofit only)
- Plays leading role in fundraising activities (nonprofit only)
- Confronts the media and community on behalf of the organization; represents organization in community
- Acts as a representative of the board as a whole, not as an individual
- Conducts evaluation of board performance with chief executive

General Board Responsibilities

- Encourages board's role in strategic planning operations
- Is a partner with chief executive in achieving mission
- Reviews with chief executive any issues of concern of the board
- Works with chief executive to ensure all board responsibilities are carried out

VICE CHAIR/VICE PRESIDENT

- Serves on executive committee
- Performs chair responsibilities when chair is unavailable
- Reports to chair of the board
- Carries out special assignments as requested by the board, such as membership, media, annual dinner, facility, or personnel
- Participates as vital part of board leadership
- Some organizations choose to make the vice chair, explicitly or implicitly, the president-elect

SECRETARY

- Serves on executive committee
- Maintains records of the board and ensures effective management and organization of records
- Manages minutes of board meetings; makes sure they are distributed to board after meetings
- Is sufficiently familiar with legal documents (articles, bylaws, IRS documents, etc.) and their applications
- Provides notice of board or committee meetings when such notice is required
- Assumes responsibilities of the president in the absence of the board president, president-elect, and vice president

TREASURER

- Serves on executive committee
- Carries out the organization's goals and objectives in relation to financial matters
- Serves as financial officer of the organization
- Serves as chair person of the finance committee; prepares agendas and year-long calendar of issues
- Works with the chief executive and chief financial officer to ensure that appropriate financial reports are made available to the board on a timely basis
- Assists the chief executive or the chief financial officer in preparing the annual budget and presenting it to the board for approval
- Reviews the annual audit and answers board members' questions about the audit
- Ensures development and board review of financial policies and procedures

- Regularly reports to board on key financial events, trends, concerns, and assessment of fiscal health
- Ensures, through the finance committee, sound management and maximization of cash and investments

BOARD MEMBER

- Regularly attends board meetings and important related meetings
- Makes serious commitment to participate in committee work
- Volunteers for and willingly accepts assignments and completes them thoroughly and on time
- Stays informed about committee matters, prepares well for meetings, and reviews and comments on minutes and reports
- Gets to know other committee members and builds a collegial working relationship that contributes to consensus
- Is an active participant in the board committees' annual evaluation and planning efforts
- Participates in fundraising for the organization (nonprofit only)

General Board Responsibilities

- Develop and implement the organization's mission and purpose
- Conduct search for executive director
- Provide support to the executive and review his or her performance
- Ensure effective organizational planning
- Ensure an adequate level of resources to conduct business
- Manage resources effectively
- Determine and monitor the organization's programs and services
- Act as liaison between organizations and public

- Serve as a court of appeal in accordance with organization's policies
- Assess its own performance in order to continuously improve performance
- Develop and take part in fundraising activities for nonprofit organizations

---

Sources:
1. Carver, J. 1997. *Reinventing Your Board: A Step by Step Guide to Implementing Policy Governance.* San Francisco: Jossey-Bass Publishers.
2. Frantzberg, A. 1997. *Not on This Board You Don't: Making Tour Trustees More Effective.* Chicago: Bonus Books.
3. Tropman, J., and E. Tropman. 1999. *Nonprofit Board: What to Do and How to Do It.* Washington, DC: Child Welfare League of America.
4. National Center for Non-Profit Boards. [Online information]. *http://www.ncnb.org.*
5. Non-Profit Managers Library. [Online information]. *http://www.mapnp.org.*
6. Support Center for Non-Profit Management—Board Café. [Online information]. *http://www.supportcenter.org*

Appendix E:
Sample Issue Briefing

PREPARED BY THE STRATEGIC
PLANNING COMMITTEE
SEPTEMBER 11, 2000

ISSUE

Whether a systemwide strategic plan is advisable or whether the system would be better served by individual plans for each of the system's major entities.

BACKGROUND

Widespan Healthcare System was formed in 1992 through the merger of First Medical Center and Cityside Hospital. The system's strategic planning process in 1995 produced two separate plans, one for each of the system's hospitals.

- Since the system's formation, the system has grown to include another hospital—Bayview Hospital—and 12 group practices, a home care program, a behavioral health program, and six outpatient clinics.
- Each of the system's owned entities has its own business plan, which is revised annually.
- Each of the hospitals in the system has its own CEO and management team.

- The system is governed by a single board, which routinely seeks input from advisory committees for each of its business units.
- For fiscal 2000, the system's profit margin was 5 percent, although one of the hospitals—Cityside—had a 2 percent margin as did the behavioral health program.
- Management of several of the system's business units—the three hospitals in particular—strongly believe they should develop strategic plans specifically for their respective operations and have voiced concerns that a systemwide plan will fail to address their specific strategic challenges.
- Because of the system's size, there has been concern voiced by the board that separate plans make tracking progress in meeting plans' objectives and identifying the need for corrective action difficult and inefficient.

KEY QUESTIONS

(Note: To the extent that the committee is prepared to provide answers to key questions, the more productive the discussion will be when it reaches the full board.)

1. Do separate strategic plans for each of the system's business units sufficiently capitalize on potential system synergies? In other words, by planning as a system could we identify opportunities that would otherwise go unidentified?
2. If we were to undertake systemwide planning, how could we address the strategic issues unique to particular operating units?
3. If we were to undertake systemwide planning would we still expect each operating unit to develop its own annual business plan? If so, what would be the relationship of these plans to the system strategic plan?
4. How do other large systems approach strategic planning?

OPTIONS

1. The system's business units should continue to conduct strategic planning independently, as well as prepare separate annual business plans.
2. We should move to a systemwide strategic planning process, but business units should continue to develop annual business plans.
3. We should move to a systemwide strategic planning process and development of a single business plan encompassing all business units.
4. The three hospitals in the system should develop a single strategic plan and another plan should be developed for other business units.

COMMITTEE RECOMMENDATION

It is our recommendation that for the planning process beginning in 2001 that we develop a systemwide plan. At the same time, in recognition of the unique strategic challenges that may face a particular operating unit, we believe that the Strategic Planning Committee should have representation from all business units. In addition, we recommend that a portion of the plan developed be reserved for articulating goals and objectives that may be applicable to only a subset (selected operating units) of the system.

Further, although we believe that the vast majority of strategic issues are truly systemwide issues, we believe that operational issues will tend to be more operating unit specific. As a result, we recommend that each operating unit should continue to develop an annual business plan.

Source: The Kahn Group, Ltd. 2000.

Appendix F:
Sample New Board Member
Orientation Agenda

JOHN C. LINCOLN HEALTH NETWORK
NEW BOARD MEMBER ORIENTATION

Person Responsible

8:00 am: Organizational Mission,
    Structure, and Overview

- History and Mission
- Corporate Structure
- Management Organization and
  Responsibilities
- Board Responsibilities
- Conflict of Interest
- Compliance
- Regulatory Agencies

8:45 am: Physician Partnerships

- Legal and Competitive Environment
- Practice Assistance
- Practice Acquisition
- Current focus of Management
  of JCL LLC

9:15 am: Managed Care

- Review of Different Kinds of
  Reimbursement
- Overview of Contracts
- Managed Care Finance
- Plan Management
- Physician Partners

10:00 am: Real Estate

- Cowden Land
- Medical Office Buildings
- Update on Current Transactions
- Confidentiality

10:30 am: Finance

- Review of Financial Statements
- Discussion of Unique Aspects of
  Health Care Finance
- Cash and Investment Management

11:15 am: Medical Staff and Quality Management

- Credentialing Process
- Board Responsibility
- Quality Improvement Reporting
- Risk Management

12:00 pm: Lunch

Source: Adapted with permission of John C. Lincoln Health
Network. 1999. Phoenix, Arizona.

Appendix G:
Sample Multirater Performance
Appraisal Instrument

THIS IS AN example of a multirater CEO performance appraisal instrument. It is not complete in that it does not include all of the questions normally asked on a CEO evaluation. Most appraisals use the computer to process the evaluation, so the rater would receive a diskette. Using the computer allows great flexibility and almost any criteria can be evaluated, such as how well the CEO or the board follows the mission statement.

Performance feedback for (Name of CEO) _____,
CEO for (Name of Organization) _____.

Name of Respondent: _____.

Return completed form NO LATER THAN: _____.

Please read instructions carefully before completing this questionnaire.

INSTRUCTIONS

Thank you for participating in the feedback process. Your time and effort are appreciated. Please give careful thought to your feedback in order to identify strengths and provide a basis for improvement. Do not rate higher or lower than deserved.

Your feedback is confidential. Your name will never be linked to the feedback you give. Other people will also contribute feedback. Your ratings will be combined (without your name) with their ratings to produce an average score, which will be summarized in a feedback report. No one can see your feedback without your password.

When writing comments describe both positive and constructive aspects. The best comments are very specific and include examples. Avoid emotional comments, whether positive or constructive. You may change your feedback at any time, even after exiting the program. Simply click on the person's name, then click "Next" to review or change your feedback.

How satisfied are you with the performance of (Name of CEO) _____, CEO for (Name of Organization) _____.

1. Involves the medical staff in planning strategy for growth of clinical services into the next century.

1	2	3	4	5	6	7	8	9	10	N/A
	Not satisfied		Minimally satisfied		Moderately satisfied		Very satisfied		Totally satisfied	

Constructive feedback: *What, if any, improvements are desired.* Please describe specifically.

_____

_____

_____

_____

2. Maintains trust by listening effectively and communicating accurately on important issues affecting medical staff.

1	2	3	4	5	6	7	8	9	10	N/A

Not satisfied	Minimally satisfied	Moderately satisfied	Very satisfied	Totally satisfied

Constructive feedback: *What, if any, improvements are desired.* Please describe specifically.

_____
_____
_____
_____

3. Is visible within the hospital and available to the medical staff and hospital personnel.

1	2	3	4	5	6	7	8	9	10	N/A

Not satisfied	Minimally satisfied	Moderately satisfied	Very satisfied	Totally satisfied

Constructive feedback: *What, if any, improvements are desired.* Please describe specifically.

_____
_____
_____
_____

4.   Conveys an understanding of the business of medical care
     delivery.

1	2	3	4	5	6	7	8	9	10	N/A

Not satisfied	Minimally satisfied	Moderately satisfied	Very satisfied	Totally satisfied

Constructive feedback: *What, if any, improvements are desired.*
Please describe specifically.

_____

_____

_____

_____

5.   Provides leadership that engenders feeling of loyalty by
     medical staff.

1	2	3	4	5	6	7	8	9	10	N/A

Not satisfied	Minimally satisfied	Moderately satisfied	Very satisfied	Totally satisfied

Constructive feedback: *What, if any, improvements are desired.*
Please describe specifically.

_____

_____

_____

_____

6. Demonstrates a value system that shows dedication to the community based on customer satisfaction, mutual respect, integrity, and creativity.

| 1 | 2 | 3 | 4 | 5 | 6 | 7 | 8 | 9 | 10 | N/A |

| Not satisfied | Minimally satisfied | Moderately satisfied | Very satisfied | Totally satisfied |

Constructive feedback: *What, if any, improvements are desired.* Please describe specifically.

_____
_____
_____
_____

7. Builds an effective management team with the consent of board.

| 1 | 2 | 3 | 4 | 5 | 6 | 7 | 8 | 9 | 10 | N/A |

| Not satisfied | Minimally satisfied | Moderately satisfied | Very satisfied | Totally satisfied |

Constructive feedback: *What, if any, improvements are desired.* Please describe specifically.

_____
_____
_____
_____

8. Supervises all business affairs and ensures that all funds are collected and expended to the best possible advantage.

1	2	3	4	5	6	7	8	9	10	N/A

Not satisfied	Minimally satisfied	Moderately satisfied	Very satisfied	Totally satisfied

Constructive feedback: *What, if any, improvements are desired.* Please describe specifically.

_____

_____

_____

_____

9. What else would you like to communicate to (Name of CEO) _____?

_____

_____

_____

_____

10. What is (Name of CEO) _____'s most outstanding asset?

_____

_____

_____

_____

11. Add any final comments that you think would be helpful
    in improving this multirater performance appraisal
    instrument.

    _____

    _____

    _____

    _____

    _____

Source: Tyler & Company. 1999.

Appendix H:
Sample CEO Job Description

Position Title: President/CEO
Department: Administration
Classification: Exempt

Job Summary: To be the direct representative of the Board of Trustees to facilitate fulfillment of the hospital's vision and mission of community service and in the management of the organization on a day-to-day basis; to act within the authority given by the Board, implementing policies as approved and coordinating the multiple activities of the hospital; and to formulate a management team of highly qualified healthcare professionals to carry out the objectives of the organization and guide the team environment for the hospital and medical staff.

Job Relationships:
Responsible to: Board of Trustees
Positions directly supervised: Vice Presidents, Director of Employee Relations, Director of Special Projects, department managers, executive assistant, medical staff coordinator, and ultimately responsible for all hospital staff.

Major Job Functions:
The following is a summary of the major essential functions of this job. The incumbent may perform other duties, both major and minor, that are not mentioned below, and specific functions may change from time to time.

1.   Develop and maintain a good working relationship with the medical staff to facilitate and ensure a collaborative and cooperative environment in carrying out the task or providing patient care.

2.   Respond to inquiries relative to policy interpretation and general administration of the hospital.

3.   Be involved in team building and development through role modeling and leadership in guests and community relations through support of the mission and vision.

4.   Ensure the continued financial viability of the hospital through prudent and efficient use of resources. Facilitate the development of annual operating and capital budget to be presented to the Finance Committee and Board before the beginning of the new fiscal year.

5.   Present annually a chart of corporate and hospital organization that supports and facilitates the vision and mission of the organization.

6.   Interpret policies and evaluate performance of management team.

7.   Support continuing performance improvement in the efficiency and effectiveness of the hospital, aiming at high quality with risk free results with involvement in legal and litigation issues.

8.   Coordinate interdepartmental functioning, responding to management requests and acting as an arbitrator between interdepartmental concerns to ensure the most efficient and effective functioning in the interest of the overall hospital.

9. Ensure that formal and informal means of communication exist for appropriate internal, interdepartmental, medical staff, Board of Trustees, and external/community communication in support of and consistent with the hospital's vision, mission, goals, and strategic initiatives.

10. Be sensitive to community relations issues by reviewing patient questionnaires, ensuring that complaints are evaluated and honestly responded to and providing input about the hospital or other healthcare issues to multiple public inquiries.

11. Act as an idea generator for newsworthy information that should be shared with the public.

12. Coordinate the multiple activities of the entire organization within the corporate structure, ensuring that there is appropriate understanding of the overall strategic objectives consistent with the hospital's vision and mission with focus on the appropriate priorities.

13. Be personally involved in related organizations, both professional and civic, as a representative of the hospital.

14. Get involved in the management of the physical plant and equipment from a decision-making perspective, ensuring that the plant is maintained and equipment is acquired within the appropriate economic resources available.

15. Represent the interest of the organization within interinstitutional state and national professional associations to affect political action and policy in the interest of the entire healthcare spectrum.

16. Maintain continuous effectiveness by participating in continuing education through seminars, reading, and networking to ensure that the techniques and skills necessary to accomplish the task are maintained and improved.

Qualifications:
The following qualifications, or equivalent, are the minimum requirements necessary to perform the essential functions of this job:

Education and formal training: Master's Degree in Health Administration.

Work experience: Five to ten years, depending on positions held
prior to being CEO.

Knowledge, skills, and abilities required: Individual must be able
to act as chief facilitator of majority of all activities of organization, must be able to analyze and react appropriately to assume
entire responsibility of organization, and must be able to cope
with level of stress and long hours.

_____   _____

Board Chairman   Date

_____

Source: Tyler & Company. 1999.

Appendix I:
Sample Board and Board Meeting
Self-Assessment Instrument

Please return the assessment before or at the next board meeting. Your responses are confidential. Check one box only.

1.   The agenda materials were:

    ☐ Excessive   ☐ Inadequate   ☐ Just right

2.   What was the most significant outcome of this meeting?

    _____

3.   What did we fail to accomplish? Why did we fail to accomplish it?

    _____

4.   On a scale of 1 to 5—1 being "Not Worthwhile" and 5 being "Highly Worthwhile"—how worthwhile was this meeting in terms of:

- Valuable discussion   _____
- Furthering the organization's mission   _____
- Positive outcomes   _____

5. On a scale of 1 to 5—1 being "Very Poor" and 5 being "Excellent"—how would you rate the following:

- Your personal contributions to the meeting   _____
- Other board members' contributions   _____
- Your preparation for the meeting   _____
- Other board members' preparation   _____

6. On a scale of 1 to 5—1 being "Very Poor" and 5 being "Excellent"—how would you rate the board chair's effectiveness at:

- Engaging board members in meaningful discussion   _____
- Challenging the board by asking the "tough questions"   _____
- Keeping the meeting focused and on track   _____
- Handling dissension   _____

7. List one thing that would have made this a better meeting.

   _____

8. Other comments

   _____

   _____

Source: The Kahn Group, Ltd. 2000.

Appendix J:
ACHE's Model CEO Employment Contract (Long Form)

This agreement, made and effective as of the _____ day of _____, 20___, between (name of Hospital), a corporation, and (name of CEO).

WHEREAS, the Hospital desires to secure the services of the CEO and the CEO desires to accept such employment.

NOW THEREFORE, in consideration of the material advantages accruing to the two parties and the mutual covenants contained herein, and intending to be legally and ethically bound hereby, the Hospital and the CEO agree with each other as follows:

1. The CEO will render full-time professional services to the Hospital in the capacity of Chief Executive Officer of the Hospital corporation. He will at all times, faithfully, industriously and to the best of his ability, perform all duties that may be required of him by virtue of his position as Chief Executive Officer and all duties set forth in Hospital bylaws and in policy statements of the Board. It is understood that these duties shall be substantially the same as those of a chief executive officer of a business corporation. The CEO is hereby vested with authority to act on behalf of

the Board in keeping with policies adopted by the Board, as amended from time to time. In addition, he shall perform in the same manner any special duties assigned or delegated to him by the Board.

2. In consideration for these services as Chief Executive Officer, the Hospital agrees to pay the CEO a salary of $ _____ per annum or such higher figure as shall be agreed upon at an annual review of his compensation and performance by the Board. This annual review shall occur three months prior to the end of each year of the contract for the express purpose of considering increments. The amount of $ _____ shall be payable in equal monthly installments throughout the contract year. The CEO may elect, by proper notice given to the Hospital prior to the commencement of any calendar year, to defer such portion of his salary to the extent permitted by the law for such year to such date as he may designate in the notice of election, such deferred amounts to be credited with periodic interest in accordance with policies established by the Hospital.

3. (a) The CEO shall be entitled to _____ weeks of compensated vacation time in each of the contract years, to be taken at times mutually agreed upon between him and the Chairman of the Board.

(b) In the event of a single period of prolonged inability to work due to the result of a sickness or an injury, the CEO will be compensated at his full rate pay for at least _____ months from the date of the sickness or injury.

(c) In addition, the CEO will be permitted to be absent from the Hospital during working days to attend professional meetings and to attend to such outside professional duties in the health-care field as have been mutually agreed upon between him and the Chairman of the Board. Attendance at such approved meetings and accomplishment of approved professional duties shall be fully compensated service time and shall not be considered vacation time. The Hospital shall reimburse the CEO for all expenses incurred by the CEO incident to attendance at approved professional meetings and such entertainment expenses incurred by the CEO in furtherance of the Hospital's interests, provided, however, that such reimbursement is approved by the Chairman of the Board.

(d) In addition, the CEO shall be entitled to all other fringe benefits to which all other employees of the Hospital are entitled.

4. The Hospital agrees to pay dues to professional associations and societies and to such service organizations and clubs of which the CEO is a member, approved by the Chairman of the Board as being in the best interests of the Hospital.

5. The Hospital also agrees to:

(a) insure the CEO under its general liability insurance policy for all acts done by him in good faith as Chief Executive Officer throughout the term of this contract;

(b) provide, throughout the term of this contract, a group life insurance policy for the CEO in an amount equivalent to $ _____, payable to the beneficiary of his choice;

(c) provide comprehensive health and major medical health insurance for the CEO and his family;

(d) purchase travel accident insurance covering the CEO in the sum of $ _____;

(e) furnish, for the use of the CEO, an automobile, leased or purchased at the beginning of alternate fiscal years, and reimburse him for expenses of its operation; and

(f) contribute on behalf of the CEO to a retirement plan qualified under the Internal Revenue Code, at the rate of $_____ per month.

6. The Board may at its discretion terminate the CEO's duties as Chief Executive Officer. Such action shall require a majority of vote of the entire Board and become effective upon written notice to the CEO or at such later time as may be specified in said notice. After such termination, all rights, duties and obligations of both parties shall cease except that the Hospital shall continue to pay the CEO his then monthly salary for the month in which his duties were terminated and for 24 consecutive months thereafter as an agreed upon severance payment. During this period, the CEO shall not be required to perform any duties for the Hospital or come to the Hospital. Neither shall the fact that the CEO seeks, accepts and undertakes other employment during this period affect such payments. Also, for the period during which such payments are being made, the Hospital agrees to keep the CEO's group life, health and major medical insurance coverage paid up and in effect, and the CEO shall be entitled to outplacement services offered by the Hospital. The severance arrangements described in this paragraph will not be payable in the event that the CEO's employment is terminated due to the fact that the CEO has been charged with any felony criminal offense related to substance abuse or to the operation of the Hospital.

7. Should the Board in its discretion change the CEO's duties or authority so it can reasonably be found that the CEO is no longer performing as the Chief Executive Officer of the Hospital and/or

its parent corporation, the CEO shall have the right, within 90 days of such event, in his complete discretion, to terminate this contract by written notice delivered to the Chairman of the Board. Upon such termination, the CEO shall be entitled to the severance payment described in Paragraph 6, in accordance with the same terms of that paragraph.

8. If the Hospital is merged, sold or closed, the CEO may terminate his employment at his discretion or be retained as President of the Hospital or any successor corporation to or holding company of the Hospital. If the CEO elects to terminate his employment at such time, he shall be entitled to the same severance arrangement as would be applicable under Paragraph 6 if the Hospital had terminated his employment at such time. Any election to terminate employment under this Paragraph must be made prior to the Hospital's merger, sale or closure, as applicable. If the CEO continues to be employed by the Hospital or its successor organization, all of the terms and conditions of this Agreement shall remain in effect. The Hospital agrees that neither it nor its present or any future holding company shall enter into any agreement that would negate or contradict the provisions of this Agreement.

9. Should the CEO at his discretion elect to terminate this contract for any other reason than as stated in Paragraph 7, he shall give the Board 90 days' written notice of his decision to terminate. At the end of the 90 days, all rights, duties and obligations of both parties to the contract shall cease and the CEO will not be entitled to severance benefits.

10. If an event described in Paragraph 6, 7, or 8 occurs and the CEO accepts any of the severance benefits or payments described therein, to the extent not prohibited by law, the CEO shall be deemed to voluntary release and forever discharge the Hospital

and its officers, directors, employees, agents, and related corporations and their successors and assigns, both individually and collectively and in their official capacities (hereinafter referred to collectively as "Releasees"), from any and all liability arising out of his employment and/or the cessation of said employment. Nothing contained in this paragraph shall prevent the CEO from bringing an action to enforce the terms of this Agreement.

11. The CEO shall maintain confidentiality with respect to information that he receives in the course of his employment and not disclose any such information. The CEO shall not, either during the term of employment or thereafter, use or permit the use of any information of or relating to the Hospital in connection with any activity or business and shall not divulge such information to any person, firm, or corporation whatsoever, except as may be necessary in the performance of his duties hereunder or as may be required by law or legal process.

12. During the term of his employment and during the 24-month period following termination of his employment, the CEO shall not directly own, manage, operate, join, control, or participate in or be connected with, as an officer, employee, partner, stockholder or otherwise, any other hospital, medical clinic, integrated delivery system, health maintenance organization, or related business, partnership, firm, or corporation (all of which hereinafter are referred to as "entity") that is at the time engaged principally or significantly in a business that is, directly or indirectly, at the time in competition with the business of the Hospital within the service area of the Hospital. The service area is defined as [describe by counties, zip codes, a mileage radius, etc.]. Nothing herein shall prohibit the CEO from acquiring or holding any issue of stock or securities of any entity that has any securities listed on a national securities exchange or quoted in a daily listing of over-the-counter market securities, provided that

any one time the CEO and members of the CEO's immediate family do not own more than one percent of any voting securities of any such entity. This covenant shall be construed as an agreement independent of any other provision of this Agreement, and the existence of any claim or cause of action, whether predicted on this Agreement or otherwise, shall not constitute a defense to the enforcement by the Hospital of this covenant. In the event of actual or threatened breach by the CEO of this provision, the Hospital shall be entitled to an injunction restraining the CEO from violation or further violation of the terms thereof.

13. The CEO shall not directly or indirectly through his own efforts, or otherwise, during the term of this Agreement, and for a period of 24 months thereafter, employ, solicit to employ, or otherwise contract with, or in any way retain the services of any employee or former employee of the Hospital, if such individual has provided professional or support services to the Hospital at any time during this Agreement without the express written consent of the Hospital. The CEO will not interfere with the relationship of the Hospital and any of its employees and the CEO will not attempt to divert from the Hospital any business in which the Hospital has been actively engaged during his employment.

14. Terms of a new contract shall be completed, or the decision made not to negotiate a new contract made, not later than the end of the tenth month. This contract and all its terms and conditions shall continue in effect until terminated.

15. This contract constitutes the entire agreement between the parties and contains all the agreements between them with respect to the subject matter hereof. It also supersedes any and all other agreements or contracts, either oral or written, between the parties with respect to the subject matter hereof.

16. Except as otherwise specifically provided, the terms and conditions of this contract may be amended at any time by mutual agreement of the parties, provided that before any amendment shall be valid or effective it shall have been reduced to writing and signed by the Chairman of the Board and the CEO.

17. The invalidity or unenforceability of any particular provision of this contract shall not affect its other provisions, and this contract shall be construed in all respects as if such invalid or unenforceable provisions had been omitted.

18. This agreement shall be binding upon the Hospital, its successors and assigns, including, without limitation, any corporation into which the Hospital may be merged or by which it may be acquired, and shall inure to the benefit of the CEO, his administrators, executors, legatees, heirs and assigns.

19. This agreement shall be construed and enforced under and in accordance with the laws of the State of _____.

This contract signed this _____ day of _____, 20___.

(NAME OF HOSPITAL)

WITNESS: _____ BY: _____
(Chairman of the Board)

WITNESS: _____ BY: _____
(CEO)

Source: American College of Healthcare Executives. 2000. Model Chief Executive Officer Employment Contract. [Online information; retrieved 6/30/00]. www.ache.org/newclub/career/sampCEO.

Appendix K:
Sample CEO Succession Planning Process

1. *Compensation Committee*
   The most appropriate group of the board to consider succession planning for the CEO is the existing Compensation Committee. Each year at this mid-year meeting (when the agenda is not quite as full as the winter meeting), the Compensation Committee should annually review and/or update the Succession Plan with the CEO. Changes, modifications and updates should be incorporated into the Plan by the CEO on an ongoing and annual basis.

2. *Memorial Health System's Strategic Plan*
   The Strategic Plan is the fundamental building block to the CEO Succession Plan. The Health System's strategic direction, changing environmental factors, and competitive dynamics will heavily influence the type of successor chosen to implement the Strategic Plan and lead the organization in both a short-term transition period as well as into the future. Particular attention should be focused on the new skills, knowledge, and personality needed to lead a rapidly changing organization in a more highly competitive environment. Especially important will be

the environmental trends and strategic themes that are an integral part of the Strategic Plan.

3.   *CEO Specifications and Profile*
The CEO job specifications and personality profile need to be determined for both the longer-term successor as well as for an interim/transition basis. The following factors are the most common and important:

For an interim/transition period during the search process for the successor CEO, stability and an orderly search process are the essential immediate needs. The search process generally takes 6–9 months before the permanent successor CEO is in place, so the board has to be concerned about sustaining momentum, preserving relationships and a smooth transition with the existing management team.

Education Background—MHA/MBA, also MD
Prior Experience—5+ years as a CEO
Visibility/Reputation—nationally (vs. regional/local)
Greatest Strengths—visionary (vs. operations)
New Skills/Knowledge—managed care and physician practice management
Background Skills/Knowledge—acute care operations, quality improvement, medical staff relationships
Other Factors—good speaking/writing skills, community health improvement, innovation and creativity, and high community visibility

4.   *Potential Internal Candidates*
The group of potential internal candidates is not large but is talented and fairly experienced. Attached is a list of the strengths and weaknesses of two potential candidates.

There are no other internal candidates that I believe could serve well in an acting role nor would be interested in being a CEO candidate during the search process.

5. *Internal Skills Development Plan*
   (To be discussed with Compensation Committee)

Source: Adapted with permission of Memorial Health System. 1999. South Bend, Indiana.

About the Authors

J. Larry Tyler, FACHE, is president of Tyler & Company, and executive search firm headquartered in Atlanta, with offices in Philadelphia, St. Louis, and Charlotte. Mr. Tyler primarily conducts CEO searches for hospitals across the United States. He began his career in search in 1978 and has conducted over 125 CEO searches. In 1995, he was cited by his peers as one of the top search consultants in the United States in the book *The New Career Makers* by John Sibbald.

Mr. Tyler is a Fellow of the American Association of Healthcare Consultants where he served in 1994–95 as chairman of the board. In 1989, he was named recipient of the Association's Chet Minkalis Service Award. He is also a Fellow of the American College of Healthcare Executives where he served as chairman of the Career Development Committee from 1994 to 1996. In 1996, he received the ACHE's Regents Award for the state of Georgia. He is Fellow of the Healthcare Financial Management Association where he is a member of the Editorial Advisory Board of *Healthcare Financial Management* magazine. He is a member of the American Institute of CPAs and the Georgia Society of CPAs.

Mr. Tyler is a noted author and lecturer. He has written over 50 articles and his book, *Tyler's Guide: The Healthcare Executive's Job Search*, was first published in May of 1994 by Health Administration Press and is now in its second printing.

Mr. Tyler has been on the ACHE Congress on Healthcare Management every year for the past 15 years and is a regular lecturer to boards of trustees.

Errol L. Biggs, PH.D., FACHE, is director, Center for Health Administration, and director, Programs in Health Administration, University of Colorado. Dr. Biggs' primary research and consulting activities include working with hospitals and medical group practices to improve governance of those organizations. He teaches governance in the graduate "on-campus" program and the Executive Program in Health Administration at the University of Colorado. Dr. Biggs has been involved in both the investor-owned and nonprofit hospital industry, having been the CEO for 12 years of large teaching hospitals.

Additionally, Dr. Biggs is a Fellow in the American College of Healthcare Executives, having served on several major committees. He is also a member of the Association of University Programs in Health Administration and Medical Group Management Association.

Dr. Biggs has served on several nonprofit as well as investor-owned boards of directors. He also directed the first merger of an osteopathic (D.O.) hospital and an allopathic (M.D.) hospital in the United States.